Psyc.

THE EXTRA-SENSORY MIND

CARMELITE MONASTERY
LIBRARY
SARANAC LAKE, N.Y.

By Kenneth Walker

THE MYSTIC MIND

THE EXTRA-SENSORY MIND

The Extra-sensory Mind

KENNETH WALKER

PERENNIAL LIBRARY

Harper & Row, Publishers

New York, Evanston, San Francisco, London

133.8
Wa E

THE EXTRA-SENSORY MIND

Copyright © 1961 by Kenneth Walker.

All rights reserved. Printed in the United States of America. No part of this book may be used or reproduced in any manner without written permission except in the case of brief quotations embodied in critical articles and reviews. For information address Harper & Row, Publishers, Inc., 49 East 33rd Street, New York, N.Y. 10016.

First PERENNIAL LIBRARY edition published 1972.

STANDARD BOOK NUMBER: 06–080248–0

Contents

Preface

IN the Preface to one of his books Dr. J. B. Rhine of Duke University, North Carolina, talks of 'the new world which the scientists are now discovering, a region within what we call the mind, a world that has been shrouded in dark mystery and superstition'. Dr. Rhine is of course referring to that part of the mind which he himself has been exploring with such conspicuous success during the last twenty years, and he is correct in describing it as being a 'world shrouded in mystery and superstition'. His sole mis-statement – and he corrects it later on in his preface – is in calling this 'a new world', for it is a world over which the magician and the priest have presided for at least ten thousand years. The only novelty lies in the fact noted by Rhine that the advanced guard of the scientists, the parapsychologists, have now set foot on this ancient territory and are claiming it to be their own.

Not that the scientists are entirely united in their approval of this movement of their advanced parties into a world which is still too shrouded in mystery and superstition to be congenial to scientists. Many of them are very uncomfortable about it and they are looking upon the reports issued, from time to time, by the parapsychologists with the gravest suspicion and disdain. This is quite understandable for references to ancient magic are to be found in these reports. As will be seen later, one of the requirements of the new radiesthesia practitioners, is that they should receive a drop of the patient's blood or saliva in order that they may make contact with him, even when he is absent. This is a relic of that ancient form of magic known as sympathetic magic. It is based on the general principle that what has once formed *part* of a *whole* still remains linked with that *whole* even after it has been forcibly separated from it. We need not be surprised therefore that the orthodox scientists are looking with very grave suspicion on the investigations being made by the parapsychologists and are even critical of the people who are displaying interest in what the parapsychologists are doing.

In a Presidential address given to the Zoological Section of the British Association in 1949, Sir Alister Hardy drew attention to the difficulties occasioned to many scientists by this advance of some of their colleagues into territories formerly under the jurisdiction of the magicians and the priests. 'There is another matter', he said 'which I feel it is only right to mention, if one is not to be intellectually dishonest. There has appeared on the horizon something which many of us do not like to look at. If it is pointed out to us, we say: "No, it can't be there, our doctrines say it is impossible." I refer to telepathy – the communication of one mind with another by means other than the special senses. I believe that no one who examines the evidence with an unbiased mind can reject it. It is perhaps unorthodox for a zoologist to introduce such a topic; but I do so for a reason. If telepathy has been established, as I believe it has, such a revolutionary discovery should make us keep our minds open to the possibility that there may be so much more in living things and their evolution than our science has hitherto led us to expect.'

As a medical man and one who is particularly interested in the psychic factors in illness, I, like Professor Hardy, feel that it is important that we should examine very carefully the work which has been done by the parapsychologists during the last twenty years. Admittedly there is much in their findings which conflicts with observations made in other fields of science but, as I have tried to show in the last chapter of this book, this lack of agreement is much less serious than at first sight it appears to be. All that is needed to rectify matters is that the scientists should waive certain assumptions which they have based on quite insufficient grounds, and that the new data provided by parapsychologists should be examined in as unprejudiced a manner as possible. That a detached and unbiased attitude to this new material is highly necessary is being amply demonstrated by certain critics of the parapsychologists. Dr. George H. Price of Minnesota is an example of this. He has declared that: 'Not one thousand experiments, with 10,000,000 trials and by one hundred separate investigators giving total odds against chance of $10/^{1000}$ to one, would induce him to accept the phenomena of extra sensory perception.'!

I am fully aware of the fact that by writing a book, of the character of this one, I am rendering myself liable to being dubbed a crank and an eccentric by my medical colleagues, but I am quite willing to take this risk. The reader will find that all that I have been guilty of doing is to have collected together a number of different observations and to have drawn certain conclusions from them. I can provide no personal guarantee of the accuracy of many of the observations I have recorded, and admittedly some of them are very surprising. All that I am able to state is that they have been made by highly intelligent and seemingly responsible people, and consequently that they are worthy of very serious consideration. This applies particularly to the unorthodox methods of diagnosis and treatment placed under the heading of radiesthesia and dealt with in Chapter 8. I had hoped that a very eminent physician would have written a foreword to this book but after reading it he decided that although he agreed with the great majority of the conclusions I had reached, the contribution of a foreword would imply that he gave his professional sanction to all that the experts in radiesthesia and radionics were attempting to do. For this reason he had to decline my invitation to contribute a foreword. I entirely understand how the physician in question reached this decision and I would like to make it quite clear in this preface that I can supply no warranty of the genuineness of the results claimed by the practitioners in radiesthesia and radionics. I look upon the present popularity of these methods of diagnosis and treatment as an exceedingly interesting phenomenon which may represent nothing more important than a reaction against the materialism and mechanism of the age. The only other comment on the methods of the radiesthesia experts I should like to make is that even when positive results have followed their use, the official explanations of how these results were obtained are not necessarily the correct explanations. Personally I regard both the methods and the results as being usually psychic in origin and as only very indirectly connected with the physical apparatus employed.

Only one more statement need be made in this Preface. It is customary for an author to produce his testimonials, in other words to refer to the various qualifications which render him a particularly suitable person to deal with the subjects he has chosen to write about. Let me confess at once that I am not an expert in any of the subjects with which I have dealt in this book. By this I mean that I possess no psychic powers, have never seen anything more startling than a make-shift apparition, readily explained in terms of moving shadows, and have no personal experience of telepathy or clairvoyance to report. In view of all these negatives it can be seen that I am very far from being either a 'medium' or a 'clairvoyant'. In the ordinary way these negative qualities of mine would render me a highly unsuitable person to write about the subjects dealt with in this book, but in my opinion, my very deficiencies now become assets to me. The fact that I have never met a ghost reduces the likelihood of my accepting the existence of ghosts on insufficient grounds. The fact that I have no psychic powers makes me examine very critically the claims made by those who possess them in a high degree. And if, having scrutinized carefully the evidence provided by the exponents of the various parapsychological activities dealt with in this book, I finally accept them as genuine phenomena, then my verdict is likely to carry much more weight with my readers than it would have done had I been either a medium or a clairvoyant.

I should also like it to be known that I have been an interested spectator only of the methods of diagnosis and of treatment grouped under the general headings of radiesthesia and radionics. I am not in a position either to reject or to support the claims which have been made for these unorthodox methods. In my opinion, all that can really be said with any confidence on this subject is that the radiesthesia movement is a very widely spread movement and that I find it difficult to dismiss the many successes claimed for it by intelligent and highly responsible people as being merely the products of their imaginations.

KENNETH WALKER

Acknowledgements

I would like to express my thanks to the many experts in fields of research of which, prior to the writing of this book, I had no knowledge at all. Without their advice and their personal interest I would probably have gone astray and I would like to make special acknowledgement of the help given by the following: Colonel K. W. Merrylees, Dr. George Lawrence, Dr. T. T. B. Watson, Dr. Eric Perkson and Allison Barnard.

I have acknowledged my indebtedness to a large number of writers in my text but certain books have been of outstanding service to me, so that I should like to mention them here at the beginning of my work.

The Personality of Man by G. N. M. Tyrell; *New Frontiers of the Mind*, *The Reach of the Mind* and *New World of the Mind*, all by J. B. Rhine; *This World and That* by Payne and Bendit; *An Experiment with Time* by J. W. Dunne; *Modern Experiments in Telepathy* by G. E. Soal and F. Bateman; *The Sixth Sense* by Rosalind Heywood; *Telepathy and Medical Psychology* by J. Ehrenwald; and various volumes of the *Proceedings of the S.P.R.* and of the *Journal of the British Society of Dowsers*.

The Unconscious Mind

This book is concerned with certain psychic phenomena which the psychologists have been too busy to report upon. It deals with those little understood functions of man's Unconscious mind which, because they appear to be exceptional, have been separated off from ordinary psychology and placed in the category of 'parapsychological phenomena'. But, as will be seen later, it is a mistake to regard such manifestations of the mind as inspiration, telepathy, precognition and clairvoyance as paranormal or exceptional, for when we come to study them we find that all of us are capable of displaying them in varying degrees. That they are looked upon as being out of the ordinary is accounted for by two facts. The first is that the other activities of our minds are so much more in evidence that we fail to take notice of the intervention, from time to time, of these underlying and much less apparent faculties. The second reason for our regarding these phenomena as being unusual is that they have not yet been accepted by the scientists as genuine phenomena. We live in a scientific age in which it is assumed that acceptable knowledge has to reach us *indirectly* through the gateway of the special senses and never *directly*, as Extra-Sensory Perception comes to us. And, of course, it is indeed true that almost all of knowledge reaches us in this indirect way and that science is entirely based on what is known as 'sense data' followed by reasoning.

For example, when I pick up an apple and examine it my senses of sight, touch, smell and taste are stimulated by it. Nervous impulses speed along a number of different sensory nerves to the headquarters of these senses in my brain, complicated physico-chemical and electrical processes are evoked there, and I obtain certain sensory information about the nature of the apple. The road by which this knowledge has reached me is an exceedingly complicated and indirect one and my conclusions concerning the apple are admittedly highly inferential in character.

But there is a much more direct way of obtaining knowledge, namely the way in which we investigate the nature of the world which lies *within us*, the world of perceptions, thoughts, memories, convictions and feelings. When we direct our attention inwards instead of outwards we establish *immediate* and *direct* contact with the contents of what we call our 'minds', and as Eddington has rightly said, they are 'the first and the most direct things in our experience'. So also is the extra-sensory knowledge which is said to reach a person through the action of inspiration, telepathy and clair-voyance of an equally direct and immediate kind, and if we are to understand ourselves and the way in which we work better it is essential that we should study the so-called paranormal phenomena of our minds much more fully than we have hitherto done. This will entail our finding answers to three preliminary questions: 'Do such extra-sensory phenomena as precognition, telepathy and clairvoyance actually exist and can they be demonstrated?' 'If they are true phenomena and are not merely figments of our imaginations, as many people appear to believe they are, can they be accounted for by accident alone?' And finally: 'If coincidence is not able to explain these phenomena, what is their true cause?'

All of these questions have been the object of very exacting research during the last fifty years and much new light has been thrown on them. Scientific methods of investigating them have been used wherever this has been possible but, it has to be realized that the human *psyche* is a very delicately balanced instrument and that it cannot be subjected to the laboratory régime and the scientific handling to which an apple can be subjected without being affected by them. Consequently the extent to which the human *psyche* can be made an object of scientific investigation is limited. This will be revealed later in this book but before the painstaking work carried out on such phenomena as Telepathy and Extra-Sensory Perception can be described it will be necessary to say something about psychological research as a whole.

As has been pointed out, the extent to which the human *psyche* can be made an object of scientific study is limited, and this means that psychology has not yet become a science. William James denied that it had even reached the stage of holding out a promise of becoming a science and all that can as yet be claimed for psychology is that it has freed itself from the restrictions formerly imposed on it by theology and that it has made great progress during the last half-century. I am, of course, referring here to the Western school of psychology, for in the East, religion, psychology and philosophy have always maintained contact with each other and they may be looked upon as being complementary studies. Consequently there is no need for Eastern psychology to bring its findings into line with the findings of religion for they have never deviated from them. In the West the situation is, and has always been, entirely different. In the Middle Ages the theologians laid down what people had to believe on the subject of the human *psyche* and what they had to reject, on the grounds that it was contrary to Church teaching. They proclaimed that man was a triad of body, mind and spirit and that man's spirit was immortal. But if anybody had had the temerity to inquire of his spiritual adviser what was the precise relationship between these three constituents of man, it is very doubtful whether he would have received an intelligible answer, not necessarily because the priest was unwilling to enlighten him but because he was as ignorant on this subject as was the questioner himself. In other words the terms 'soul', 'mind' and 'spirit' have never been satisfactorily defined by the Church and nobody knows in what relationship these three entities stand to each other.

But at the dawn of the Age of Science, in the seventeenth century, men were no longer content to leave everything in the hands of the theologians and, amongst the subjects into which they began to inquire, were the subjects of knowledge and the way in which knowledge was acquired. At the start it was the philosophers who were responsible for the study of these subjects, and particularly such philosophers as Locke, Berkeley, Hume and Kant. It was not until the close of the nineteenth century that psychologists, in the true sense of that word, began to appear on the scene, and mainly in Germany, France and Great Britain. It is beyond the scope of this book to give an account of the rise, the development and the spread of the Western school of psychology, and we shall confine our attention entirely to those individual members of the Western school who have contributed most to our understanding of the part of the mind in which we are at present interested – the *Unconscious Mind*.

The Nature of the Unconscious Mind

Few statements are less accurate than the statement sometimes made to the effect that it was Freud who first discovered the Subconscious and Unconscious areas of the mind, for the existence of these regions was recognized by the Mystics and the neo-Platonists long before any professional psychologists appeared on the scene. For example, we find William Law describing a great underground current of thoughts, wishes and emotions which swept along in the darker regions of man's mind, a current which had a very marked effect on his conduct and his thinking. So also, in 1886, did the Cambridge Platonist Dallas write: 'In the dark recesses of memory, in unbidden suggestions, in trains of thought unwittingly pursued, in multiplied waves and currents . . . in dreams that cannot be laid, in the forces of instinct . . . we have glimpses of a great tide of life, ebbing and flowing, rippling and rolling, and beating about where we cannot see it.' The Puritans were particularly familiar with this great underground flow of unbidden and sinful suggestions and they regarded it as being the voice of the Devil speaking within them.

Freud's great contribution to our understanding of the Unconscious Mind was his discovery that stresses and conflicts in this region of the *psyche* are often the source of illnesses, and that by bringing these unseen difficulties up from the Unconscious Mind into the area of consciousness, so that they can be clearly seen by the patient, the illness is often relieved. The means by which this is brought about is psycho-analysis, and in the course of using this valuable method of exploring the Unconscious Mind, Freud made an additional discovery of great importance. He realized that his own efforts to dig down into the troubled areas of his patient's Unconscious were being thwarted by strong opposition on his patient's part: it was as though the less unconscious layers of his mind were actively resisting his attempts to find out what lay beneath them. Freud revealed his genius by tumbling to the fact that this opposition came from the same forces which prevented the *patient* from knowing the contents of *his own* Unconscious. In other words, the ideas hidden in his Unconscious were outcasts who had been driven away from the company of the more respectable ideas in the patient's Conscious and had been forced to take refuge in the darkness of his Unconscious.

From these observations Freud evolved what is best called a 'dynamic' conception of the human mind. He pictured it as being divided into a number of different compartments, each compartment filled with ideas existing under varying degrees of pressure. The pressure was the result of the forces which were required to keep them where they were. According to Freud, there is very little free communication between one compartment of our minds and another compartment of them. This is due to the interference of a special 'selective agent' or 'censor' who permits only certain ideas freedom to pass from one compartment to another compartment of it. The strictest form of censorship lies between the 'Unconscious' and what Freud called the 'Pre-conscious', but a subsidiary and less demanding official is stationed between the Pre-conscious and the Conscious regions. Because many of the ideas in a patient's mind are continually being subjected to this bullying by officials the pressure may become so great that the patient breaks down under the strain of it – in other words he becomes ill.

Freud drew what might be called an elevation plan of the human mind dividing it into three main floors or compartments, the *Id*, the *Ego* and the *Super-ego*. The *Id* is the dark and entirely unconscious basement of the mind in which are housed a number of primordial and instinctive urges, most of them of a sexual nature. These primitive ideas are continually struggling to find expression and they are continually being prevented from finding it by the more conscious mind, and by the extremely respectable ideas that are residing in it, just as upper floor tenants in a house do everything they can to prevent the basement tenants from trespassing upstairs.

The *Ego* is that part of the *psyche* which is usually known as the 'Personality' and the *Super-ego* is an off-shoot of the *Ego*. The *Super-ego* is the repository of the ideals and of the code of morality of the Ego. The personal ideals and values of the *Ego* are not necessarily genuine ideals and values which we have discovered and approved of ourselves. More often than not they are ideals and values which have been forced on us, whilst we were children, by our parents and our nurses. These values were undoubtedly of great service to the said parents and nurses whilst they were engaged in the difficult business of training us, but they do not necessarily reflect our own views, now that we have grown up. They may represent only that conventional code of morals which a cynic once described as being 'what your nurse told you to do, before you were old enough to know better'.

Freud's dynamic conception of the mind has proved extremely useful in medical practice. It helps to explain a neurotic patient's irrational behaviour, his ever-changing moods, his lack of unity and the incessant conflict in the depths of his mind. Freud's conception of the Unconscious also provides an excellent basis for psycho-analysis but it is far too restricted a view of the human mind to be of much help to us in interpreting the psychic phenomena which are the subject of the later chapters of this book. Freud was primarily a medical man and as such he was particularly interested in the diagnosis and the treatment of nervous diseases. He was indeed far more concerned with psycho-pathology than with normal psychology, and this being so, it will be more profitable to turn our attention to other systems of psychology with a broader outlook on the Unconscious than that of Freud.

The system which is likely to be of most service to us as a psychological background to the special phenomena

we are about to study, is the system propounded, at the
end of the Victorian Age, by Freud's predecessor,
W. H. Myers. We all approach the various objects of
our study with what may be called a 'centre of interest'
and Myers's centre of interest in psychology was the
existence of a number of different levels of consciousness.
He was particularly intrigued by the idea of a *threshold*
of consciousness, that is to say, a level of consciousness
which our thoughts and sensations have to attain before
we are able to register them. This idea of a *threshold* of
consciousness was not a new one, but Myers extended
the use of the term 'subliminal' so that it embraced
much more than had been included in it before. For
Myers, subliminal meant everything which occurred
'beneath the ordinary level of consciousness on which
we live and have our being'. He also coined the term
'subliminal event' and by this he meant all that happens
in the mind *beneath* the level of consciousness on which
the individual habitually lives. If the reader prefers a
different way of expressing the same idea, the Subliminal Self includes everything which lies 'outside the
margin of the individual's field of consciousness'.
Myers includes amongst these Extra-marginal and
Subliminal events not only 'those faint stimulations
whose very faintness keeps them submerged', but the
many events which we fail to register at all, for example
the sensations, thoughts and emotions which, though
definite and independent, 'have not as yet joined the
supraliminal current of moving, intellectual and
emotional reactions constituting our personalities'.

Having impressed upon us the fact that subliminal
events are not sporadic and intermittent episodes but

that they constitute a continuous chain of memories and reactions which he calls the Subliminal Self, Myers makes two statements. The first is that there is a constant co-operation between the quasi-independent and underground trains of thought in us and the over-lying and more conscious levels of thought. His second observation is that frequent upheavals occur in our minds, so that thoughts which were formerly far below the level of consciousness rise above it, sometimes only temporarily, but at other times for good. Myers continues his description of the different layers of the mind thus: 'Perceiving that these submerged thoughts and emotions possess the characteristics which we associate with conscious life, I feel bound to speak of a *Subliminal* or ultra-marginal consciousness.' Having placed emphasis again on the rising of subliminal thoughts and emotions from below into the super-imposed layers of consciousness, Myers expresses the view that the study of this phenomenon may throw light on the *psychic* and so-called *paranormal* functions with which this book is principally concerned. He writes: 'Telepathy and clairvoyance, or the perception of distant thought and distant scenes without the agency of the recognized organs of sense . . . these faculties suggest either an incalculable extension of our own mental powers, or else the influence upon us of minds freer and less trammelled than our own.'[1] What Myers means by the influence on us of 'minds freer than our own' will be discussed in later chapters of this book and all that need be pointed out here is that Myers's wider view of the subliminal mind and the greater interest he takes

[1] F. W. H. Myers, *Human Personality*.

in telepathy, precognition and clairvoyance renders his system of psychology a much more appropriate setting for a discussion of these subjects than the better known system of Freud.

Comparison of Myers's Subliminal Self with Freud's Unconscious

Myers's Subliminal Self differs very markedly from Freud's Unconscious and has closer affinities with the *Inconscient* of the French school of psychology, to which Richet, Janet and Bidel belonged. Myers is also one of the few Western psychologists to pay attention to the all-important fact that consciousness is a variable which fluctuates at different periods of the day and the night, so that we are sometimes much more aware of our existence and of what we are doing than we are at other times. What Freud failed to emphasize sufficiently was the fact that we spend most of our waking hours on a comparatively low level of consciousness, doing things, thinking things and feeling things without being *aware* either of ourselves or of what we are doing, thinking and feeling. But this is a fact which as yet very few Western psychologists have recognized. So also do the majority of Western psychologists take very little notice of a truth to which Myers drew attention long ago, namely 'that we employ the pronoun "I" to represent a very limited and specialized portion of what is really a much more extensive "self" '. But the most important of all the differences between the Subliminal Self of Myers and the Unconscious of Freud is that Myers was an idealist who looked upon the Subliminal Self as being the site of *higher* activities as well as of man's lower animal drives and urges. To Myers the Subliminal mind was a part of the mind in which gold as well as rubbish could be discovered by those who looked for it. Myers summarizes his description of the Subliminal Self as follows: 'I do not, by using this term, assume that there are two co-related and parallel "selves" existing always within us. Rather I mean by the "Subliminal Self" that part of the self which is commonly subliminal; and I conceive that there may be – not only co-operation between these quasi-independent trains of thought – but also upheavals and alternations of personality of many kinds, so that what was once below the surface for a time, or permanently, rises above it. And I conceive also that no self of which we can have cognizance is in reality more than a fragment of a larger self – revealed in a fashion at once shifting and limited.'

Myers draws an analogy between man's understanding of the world within himself and his understanding of the sunshine which reaches him from the sun in the form of a mixture of light and heat. He writes that awareness of his existence is presented to a child much as sunshine is presented to a man, namely, as a mixture of two entities. 'Optical analysis splits up the whole ray into the various rays which compose it. Philosophical analysis, in like manner, splits up the vague consciousness of the child into many faculties – into the various external senses, and the various modes of thought within. Experimental psychology is now adding a further refinement. In the sun's spectrum . . . are many dark lines or bands due to the absorption of certain rays by certain vapours in the atmosphere of the sun.

And similarly in the range of spectrum of our own sensations and faculties there are many inequalities of brightness and definition . . . The psychologist who observes say, how his reaction times are modified by alcohol is like the physicist who observes what lines are darkened by the interposition of a special gas.' Myers then draws our attention to the fact that the limits to the visibility of sunlight are not imposed by any restrictions on the part of the sun but by the incapacity of our own eyes to see. 'Beyond each end of the prismatic ribbon are waves of which our retinas take no cognizance.' On the far side of the red end of the spectrum are waves of sunlight whose potency we detect, not in the terms of light but in terms of heat. 'Even thus . . . *beyond* each end of our conscious spectrum extends a range of faculty and perception, exceeding the known rays, but as yet indistinctly guessed.' When Myers likens a part of the human mind to the infra-red end of the spectrum he is in all probability referring to that part of our Central Nervous System which regulates and co-ordinates the many complicated physiological processes of our bodies, activities of which we are only very dimly aware. When he likens our higher psychological activities to the ultra-violet end of the spectrum, he is suggesting that in all probability there exist in man still higher psychological processes of which we know little or nothing: 'Yet it is there,' he adds, 'there, beyond the violet, that we shall find our inquiry opening upon a cosmic prospect inciting us upon an endless way.'

Myers has provided us with a generous scheme of psychology, a scheme into which it may or may not prove possible for us to fit the psychological phenomena which are about to be studied. He has also suggested that there exist in man many other faculties of which we know little or nothing, higher states of being and higher levels of consciousness which may be the ultimate goal of humanity, but which, up till now, have been attained only by a few exceptional people. In short, Myers has provided us with a system of psychology with which it is possible for us to work.

It is with the Unconscious or Subliminal regions of the mind that we shall be chiefly concerned in the following chapters. These underground areas of the mind are scenes of intense and ceaseless activity. They are responsible for the initial stages in the production of a great many of our ideas and feelings and it is not surprising that in the earlier stages of their manufacture, these ideas and feelings are often of a rather primitive nature. They recapitulate, as it were, the earlier and more primitive eras of human thought. As the developing human embryo recapitulates in its body the earlier stages of man's physical evolution, so may it be said that the Subliminal Self recapitulates, in miniature, some of the earlier stages of man's psychic evolution. The Unconscious Mind is also a factory of dreams, a factory which never closes its doors. As Dr. Maurice Nicoll has pointed out, this part of the Subliminal Self's work, that of supplying 'fresh dramatic structures to a man who dreams every night' – as most of us really do – is no light undertaking. The Unconscious Mind also helps to produce the imaginings and daydreams in which we spend so many of our so-called waking hours. Nor is this the limit of its work. It co-ordinates the manifold physiological processes and movements of our bodies and, as we shall see later, it may also maintain a much closer contact than we imagine with the Subliminal regions of other people's minds. It is indeed the most industrious part of our minds, to which all the hardest work has been allotted, work which may be of far greater importance to our health and to our happiness than the highly publicized mental activity being carried on by the tenants who are living upstairs on the ground floor level.

2

Psychic Research and the Phenomenon of Inspiration

Before paranormal activities of the mind such as Telepathy and Clairvoyance are discussed something must be said about Psychical Research in general, for much confusion exists on this subject. Many people believe that Psychical Research and Spiritualism are closely connected but this is quite incorrect. The function of the Society for Psychical Research (S.P.R. for short) is to report upon all psychic phenomena submitted to them for investigation and amongst these phenomena are those which are said to have happened in spiritualistic séances. A careful scrutiny of these séance phenomena is particularly necessary, for the spiritualists are inclined to accept their genuineness without studying them, on the grounds that they are in harmony with their own central belief – the personality's survival of the death of the body. Consequently the S.P.R. is carrying out highly necessary work in examining critically reports coming from all sources and particularly from sources of a spiritualistic nature.

G. N. M. Tyrell, an ex-President, has given us an excellent account of the founding of the Society for Psychical Research in his Pelican book *The Personality of Man*,[1] a book to which I am very deeply indebted. In this book he records that the S.P.R. was founded at the end of the last century and that its first meeting was held in 1882. Previously there were individuals

[1] G. N. M. Tyrell, *The Personality of Man*.

who were interested in the subject of parapsychology. Most of these interested people were educated men of the high mental calibre of Professor de Morgan, Alfred Russell Wallace and Sir William Crookes, but there existed no organized group for the promotion of research. The aim which the new Society set before itself was to collect facts, to make observations and to sift evidence without, for the moment, expressing any opinion about the explanation of the facts and observations it had examined. Amongst the new members of the Society there were scientists who were of the opinion that if progress were to be made in the research on which they were embarking, it would have to be based mainly on two things, namely accurate observation and properly controlled experiments, whenever the latter were possible. Actually only two individuals amongst the founders of the S.P.R. were interested in the subject of spiritualism, namely Dr. F. W. H. Myers, the author of *Human Personality and its Survival of Death* and Henry Sidgewick, who afterwards became Knightsbridge Professor of Moral Philosophy at Cambridge. These two were old friends, for when Myers was an undergraduate reading Classics at Cambridge, Sidgewick had been his tutor. Both of them were keenly interested in the subject of the human *psyche*, and of its fate after death, and many discussions had taken place between them in their college rooms. Before parting they had made a compact with each other, that if ever an opportunity for this were to occur at a later date, they would subject psychic phenomena in general, and the claims of the spiritualists in particular, to very searching tests. Myers had been an exceptionally brilliant classical scholar and he seemed to be destined for an academic career, but later he sacrificed his classical future in order that he might fulfil the promise he had made to his old tutor. Abandoning classical studies for good he plunged with characteristic enthusiasm into the study of psychology and, within a comparatively short time, he became an authority on this subject.

Sidgewick and Myers were joined afterwards by William Barrett, by Edmund Gurney, a member of the well-known Quaker family of that name, by Sidgewick's wife, an extremely gifted woman, and by a number of Mrs. Sidgewick's distinguished relatives. Amongst these were her two brothers, Lord Arthur and Lord Gerald Balfour, and her brother-in-law, the eminent chemist, Lord Raleigh. Seldom has any society started with such a galaxy of talent as its founders as the S.P.R. did. The society held its first meeting on 17 July 1882 under the chairmanship of its President, Henry Sidgewick, a man of particularly sound judgement. It was quite impossible to have doubts about the integrity of such a Society. As Professor C. D. Broad has put it: 'It was hardly possible to maintain, without writing oneself down as an ass, that a society over which Sidgewick presided and in whose work he was actively interested, consisted of knaves and fools, concealing superstitions under the cloak of scientific verbiage.'

And it was particularly necessary that a society engaged in such research as this should be run by people of complete integrity and of exceptionally sound judgement, for at that time scientists and even most educated people looked upon psychic phenomena of every kind with the very gravest suspicion. So sceptical were the majority of educated people that a man or woman who displayed an interest in such matters ran a serious risk of being dismissed as a crank by his friends and acquaintances. Nor has this danger to one's personal reputation entirely disappeared at the present time, in spite of our greater knowledge of psychology and parapsychology. The author of this book recalls inquiring of a professional colleague a few years ago, whether he believed or not in the existence of telepathy and his colleague's reply was: 'Yes, I do, but for heaven's sake, don't mention it to anybody, for I don't want to lose my practice.' His caution was fully justified for the medical profession is inclined to look askance at anything which may have an element of quackery in it and it has always been scared of new and unproven methods of treatment. At the end of the last century Hypnotism, or what was then called Mesmerism, met the strongest opposition from medical men and a special committee of scientists and physicians was appointed in order to investigate this phenomenon. The Committee returned a very unfavourable verdict on hypnotism, dismissing it as a fraud and a menace. *The Lancet* was particularly outspoken on this subject and it expressed the strongest disapproval of everybody who had shown any interest in it, ending its comment with the following anathema: 'We regard the abettors of Mesmerism as quacks and impostors; they ought to be hooted out of professional society.'

Fortunately there were a few medical men who were bold enough to continue their investigations of hypnotism in the face of *The Lancet's* stern warning. It became known a few years later that Mr. Esdaile, surgeon to the Calcutta Hospital, had performed a great many operations successfully with his patients under hypnosis and eventually the medical profession was forced to acknowledge that 'there must be something in it'. It is interesting to note that when eventually hypnotism was accepted as a genuine phenomenon, it was regarded as being an unusual and exceptional manifestation of the human *psyche*, in the same way that clairvoyance and telepathy are now considered to be *paranormal* or unusual phenomena. This attitude to hypnotism has, of course, now been abandoned and a similar change may eventually be made in our attitude to clairvoyance and telepathy. Instead of being called paranormal they will be accepted as being phenomena of which everybody is potentially capable.

The Phenomena of Inspiration

The paranormal phenomena which has been most widely accepted as genuine and for the existence of which there is now the clearest evidence is the phenomenon of inspiration. The great majority of writers on this subject accept the view that inspiration, whether it be that of the poet, the musician, the painter, the saint, the prophet or the scientist, originates below in Myers's subliminal regions of the mind, and thence rises up to the level of consciousness, knocking, as it were, at the door of awareness for admittance. This means that the more conscious level of the mind is not the actual creator of the inspired message but is only its agent and its interpreter. The fact that inspiration comes from an unconscious region of the mind accounts for its widely recognized characteristic, the feeling which accompanies it that it has been delivered as a whole, and only in need of being formulated and expressed. Every inspired person, whether he be a highly gifted poet, musician, saint, prophet or scientist, or only an ordinary man or woman, has laid stress on the *given* nature of the message. That poetry was a gift from elsewhere was amongst the final utterances of the poet Blake, as he lay dying. He had been restless and even during his last hours he had been reaching out for a pencil and paper so that his wife besought him not to exhaust himself by writing poetry, but to rest. 'But it is not mine; it is not mine,' he cried, still seeking to put down on paper the poem he had received, before it faded and was lost for ever.

So also does the inspired musician feel that the music he is attempting to record is not his own music but something which has come to him from an outside source, so that his sole responsibility lies in putting it down on paper as faithfully as he can. Not that this is in any way a light undertaking. On the contrary, the writing of the poem or the music may, and often does, entail for the poet or musician, a tremendous struggle. Shelley is repeatedly calling attention to the suddenness and to the joy associated with inspiration as when, in his *Hymn to Intellectual Beauty*, he exclaims:

> 'Sudden the shadow fell on me;
> I shrieked and clasped my hands in ecstasy.'

So also does Shelley declare that no man can say 'I will write poetry'. Not even the greatest poet is able to do that for 'poetry is not like reasoning – a power to be exerted according to the determination of the will'.

Trelawney gives us a picture of Shelley after one of these sudden attacks of inspiration. He describes how the poet had wandered off by himself into a wood near Pisa, the city in which they were living at that time, and how he had afterwards gone out in search of him. Eventually he found Shelley propped up against the trunk of a tree and surrounded by a litter of paper covered with frightful scrawls. 'Words had been smeared out with the finger and, one upon the other, over and over in tiers, and all run together . . . It might have been taken for a sketch of a marsh over-grown with bull-rushes, and the blots for wild duck; such a dash-off daub as self-conceited artists mistake for a manifestation of genius. On my observing this he answered: "When my brain gets heated with thought, it soon boils and throws off images and words faster than I can skim them off." '

Keats gives a similar account of how his description of Apollo, found in his third book of Hyperion, came to him. He states that it arrived 'by chance or magic – as if it were something given to him'. He also admits that he did not recognize how beautiful were the expressions which the description contained until after they had been transferred to paper. On reading them he was struck with astonishment, for they seemed to be the production of another person.

Robert Louis Stevenson personified the subliminal faculties which were responsible for so much of his own writings, and he called them his 'Brownies', and his 'Little People'. He tells us that whenever it became necessary for him to produce stories for publication the 'Little People who manage man's inner theatre' realized this fact as clearly and as promptly as he did himself. This meant that whenever he lay down in bed at night prepared to sleep 'he no longer sought amusement but printable and profitable tales; and after he had dozed off in his box-seat his Little People contrived their evolutions with the same mercantile design . . .' For the most part, whether awake or asleep he is simply occupied – he or his Little People – in consciously making stories for the market . . . The more I think of it the more I am moved to press upon the world the question 'Who are the Little People?' They are near connexions of the dreamer's beyond doubt; they share in his financial worries and have an eye on the Bank book; they share plainly in his training . . . they have plainly, like him, to build the scheme of a story and to arrange emotions in progressive order; only I think they have more talent; and one thing is beyond doubt – 'they can tell him a story piece by piece, like a serial, and keep him all the while in ignorance of where they aim.' He continues thus: 'That part (of my work) which is done while I am sleeping is the Brownie's part, beyond contention; but that which is done when I am up and about is by no means necessarily mine, since all goes to show that the Brownie's have a hand in it even then.'[1]

The great musicians write in a very similar manner of those moments in which inspiration bubbles up from below. Mozart laid special stress on the fact, that musical compositions were presented to him as complete wholes. 'Nor do I have in my imagination the parts *successively*, but I hear them as it were, all at once.'

[1] Quoted by F. W. H. Myers in *Human Personality*.

Then followed the exceedingly difficult work of getting down on paper and of working upon the material which had originated below in the Unconscious Mind. Georges Sand gives us a particularly vivid account of the sufferings endured by her lover, Chopin, whenever he was engaged on this tiresome work of recording what had previously been received. She narrates how he would return from a solitary walk with music 'ringing in his mind' and how there would then begin for him the torture of getting it down on paper. 'It was a series of efforts, of irresolutions and of frettings, to seize again certain details of the theme he had heard. He would shut himself up in his room for whole days, weeping, walking, breaking his pens, repeating and altering a bar a hundred times.' And Chopin might spend as long as six weeks before he succeeded in writing down the music in the form in which it had come to him.

What is true of the poets and the musicians is to a lesser extent true also of the scientists, that the solution of many of the key problems in science have come to them quite suddenly, in a flash of intuition. Lord Kelvin describes one of these fruitful moments and it is well known that the chemist, Kekulé visualized the structure of a molecule of benzene, in an instant, whilst seated on top of a bus. Into his mind there suddenly came the ancient symbol of the serpent biting its own tail, and in a flash he evolved the chemical formula of the 'benzene ring'.

But it is not only the geniuses who may experience an upsurge of messages from the unconscious regions of their minds. Quite ordinary people have described this and many examples of it are to be found in the literature of the phenomenon generally known as 'automatic writing'. This pastime, for comparatively few people have experimented with automatic writing seriously, has usually been carried out with the help of a simple contrivance known either as a 'planchette' or as an 'Ouija board'. All that this consists of is a small and perfectly smooth board, around the periphery of which are inscribed the letters of the alphabet. The automatic writer places some small flat smooth object such as a match-box on top of the board, establishes light contact with this object with the tips of his fingers and, having done this, ceases to look at the instrument or to pay any more attention to it. After a few minutes the flat object usually starts to slide automatically over the board in the direction of the various letters marked on its edges, and words may be spelt out by these means. At first, the process is a very slow one, but with a little practice the movements quicken and become more rapid than would have been possible had they been the more conscious products of the mind. After still more practice, mechanical contrivances can usually be dispensed with and all that is required of the writer is that he should hold a pencil lightly in his hand, think no more about it and allow the pencil to move as it likes.

Automatic writing and Ouija boards were by-products of the spiritualistic cult which began in America round about the year 1848. Two adolescent American girls, known as the Fox sisters, were responsible for what later became a craze. These two girls claimed that they could communicate with the spirits of deceased people by means of a code of raps and their parents were astute enough to realize that financial profit could be made out of their children's statement. As a result of the Fox family's enterprise, the spiritualistic cult spread rapidly over America and then at a later date, over Europe. In the course of time there appeared a number of professional 'mediums', who claimed that they were able to act as contact-agents between the living and the dead. They knew their way about in the after-world and could get in touch with the dead and bring back messages from them for the living. In this manner spiritualism appeared and rapidly spread. Amongst the uneducated, simple and credulous people who took part in spirit-rappings and table-turning, there were a few better educated men and women who were interested in the strange and inexplicable phenomena which undoubtedly occurred at some of the spiritualistic séances. Their investigations showed that it was not always necessary to resort to professional mediums in order to obtain unusual phenomena. It was quite possible for people to experiment with such things as table-turning and automatic writing privately in their own homes, and these spiritualistic pastimes became very popular in certain sections of America and European society. Victor Hugo and Elizabeth Browning took part in them and Browning's poem on the burial of the medium, Mr. Sludge, suggests that he did not approve of his wife's interest in spiritualism.

The Strange Case of Mrs. Curran

It was not only the intellectual and the advanced thinker who became interested in such phenomena as automatic writing. Amongst those who tried their hand at it was a certain Mrs. John H. Curran of St. Louis, Missouri, who was very far from being a high-brow. She was born of British parents who had emigrated to America in 1883 and although she was an intelligent girl she had received only a fitful education, leaving school for good at the age of fourteen. After her marriage, she lived at St. Louis and it is reported that at the age of thirty-one, she had never seen anything of the world outside that neighbourhood. Although uninterested in the wave of spiritualism which was then passing across America, Mrs. Curran was persuaded by a friend to try her hand at the popular game of automatic writing. At first the Ouija board her friend had lent her afforded her no pleasure at all, but persevering with it, she eventually became highly expert in its use. A few years later she wrote three historical novels with its help, novels which were published under the following titles: *The Sorry Tale*, *Hope Trueblood* and *Telka*. The last of the three novels was cast in medieval England and it was very widely read. Psychologically speaking, all of her books were of immense interest and they were examined by many different experts. The philologist who read *Telka* stated that ninety per cent of the words used in it by Mrs. Curran were Anglo-Saxon words and that no term had been employed which was of later origin than the eighteenth century. So also did an historian report that the social and historical background, both of *Telka* and of Mrs. Curran's first book, *The Sorry Tale*, were remarkably correct. *The Sorry Tale* was concerned with the Roman Empire, about which the conscious mind of Mrs. Curran knew nothing at all. Indeed, so unreliable was

Mrs. Curran's knowledge of history in general that she was under the impression that Henry VIII had eventually been beheaded as a punishment for having been unfaithful to so many of his wives. Yet the historians could find no errors in any of her three historical novels!

Mrs. Curran eventually attained such fame in the United States that several well-known American psychologists asked permission to examine her and, having been granted this privilege, one of them continued his psychological investigation of her for a period of over two years. His reason for doing so was that he wanted to discover the degree of intelligence which the subconscious areas of a mind were capable of displaying. His final verdict on this subject was to the effect that there existed in the subconscious region of Mrs. Curran's mind a 'subliminal self' which far outstripped her 'primary consciousness' in range, power and intelligence. Farther than this he was not prepared to go.

What explanation can be offered of this astonishing intellectual feat on the part of an ill-educated American woman, a woman who had no access to libraries and who heard very little intelligent conversation in a provincial American town? How can we account for her ability to write three novels, the historical, social and philological details of which were certified as being remarkably correct by the appropriate experts? Three possible explanations offer themselves; the explanation that Mrs. Curran derived her information telepathically from knowledgeable people; that her Unconscious Mind managed to establish contact with some common pool of knowledge of a similar nature to that which is postulated by Jung in his theory of the 'Collective Unconscious'; finally, there is the spiritualistic explanation which Mrs. Curran herself favoured, the explanation that her automatic writing was controlled by a disembodied spirit who possessed knowledge which she, Mrs. Curran, did not possess.

These three alternatives will be discussed later in this chapter and we shall start by examining the theory to which Mrs. Curran subscribed, namely the idea that she was under the tutelage of a disembodied spirit with the name of Patience Worth. Prior to embarking on automatic writing, Mrs. Curran had disclaimed all personal interest in spiritualism, yet afterwards she fell back on the explanation to which spiritualists invariably have recourse whenever they are faced with a difficult psychological problem, the idea of possession by a disembodied spirit. And to an uneducated person such as Mrs. Curran, spiritualism was the simplest and the most straightforward of the three available explanations. At any rate this was the explanation which Mrs. Curran chose and on which she acted with the utmost confidence for the rest of her life. She announced that the spirit that had taken charge of her was that of a girl named Patience Worth, who had lived during the seventeenth century at a Dorset farm but had afterwards emigrated to the New World. Patience Worth was a very different person from Mrs. Curran, not only as regards knowledge but also in character and temperament. She was a caustic, obstinate and highly gifted young woman who possessed an unusual knowledge of history, and was capable of writing novels in the vernacular at an astonishing speed. Being a very forceful character and fully aware of her own ability, Patience Worth kept the poorly educated Mrs. Curran in her right place and Mrs. Curran, realizing that she was in capable hands, responded by treating Patience Worth with the greatest respect. The relationship between the two personalities was analogous to the relationship existing between a musician or poet and the Muse which has taken charge of him. Mrs. Curran knew and accepted the fact that Patience Worth was more efficient than she was herself and she made her responsible for everything which the characters in her novels did and said. Mrs. Curran has left us the following description of the way in which the scenes and the characters in her novels were revealed to her by Patience Worth. 'The scene becomes panoramic, the characters moving and acting their parts . . . I see not only them but the neighbouring part of the street with the buildings, stones, dogs, people and all, just as they would be in a real scene. If people talk a foreign language . . . I hear the talk but, over and above all, is the voice of Patience Worth, either interpreting or giving me the part she wishes to use as a story.'

Mrs. Curran's novel, *The Sorry Tale*, contains a description of Imperial Rome during the periods when Augustus and Tiberius were Emperors, and Tyrell quotes a classical scholar's verdict on Mrs. Curran's masterly handling of Roman history: 'As to Rome, it (the book) presents the characters of Augustus and Tiberius with fidelity, though it makes that of Tiberius accord with the records of Tacitus and Suetonius, rather than with the views of modern historians. It shows an understanding of the relations between

Augustus and Tiberius, domestic as well as political. Knowledge of the broad sweep of the Roman Empire and the extent of the commerce, the social relations and customs of Rome, the slavery system, the luxury of the Imperial Court, garb and weapons of the soldiers, the contests of the arena, games and many other details of Roman Government and life is indicated in the allusions of the story . . . An acquaintance with the political relations of Rome to the Jews and with the form of Roman government in Palestine is shown. The situation of the Herodian dynasty is evidently understood and the time and the circumstances known. The character of Herod is revealed in a few lines that indicate information derived from Josephus or some unknown source.'[1]

Yet, if Mrs. Curran is to be believed, all of this historical knowledge was the product of the guidance she was receiving from Patience Worth, a simple country wench who lived in the seventeenth century, long after the Rome of which she possessed so intimate a knowledge had crumbled into ruins. In view of this it is impossible to regard Mrs. Curran's spiritualistic explanation of her novel writing as entirely satisfactory. A more plausible theory would be that Mrs. Curran herself had lived both in ancient Rome and in medieval England and that somehow or other she had managed to retain memories of her former incarnations. It is more than likely that Patience Worth represented some secondary character in Mrs. Curran's subliminal self, an unconscious part of her mind which, by one means or another, was able to make contact with other minds, or else with some common pool of ideas, the existence

[1] G. N. M. Tyrell, *The Personality of Man.*

of which is supported by Jung's theory of a Collective Unconscious. But whatever the true explanation be, it is evident from her own writings that Mrs. Curran looked upon the scholarly person within herself, whom she had christened Patience Worth, with the very greatest respect, and that she was grateful to her for supplementing the education which had come to an end so early in her own life. She expresses her appreciation of Patience Worth's services repeatedly and particularly in the following lines: 'Six years ago I could not have understood the literature of Patience Worth, had it been shown to me . . . The sensation of the presence of Patience is one of the most beautiful sensations that it can be the privilege of the human being to experience.'

It has been suggested by certain critics that, quite unknown to the experts who had examined her and to her relatives and her friends, Mrs. Curran had managed to haunt libraries and to ram her mind with information about the historical periods in which her future novels were to be cast. But we possess so much knowledge of Mrs. Curran's life, from her childhood onwards, and she was examined so thoroughly by her three psychologists, that this is a highly improbable explanation of her novel writing. Neither the spiritualistic nor the split personality theory of the authorship of Mrs. Curran's novels are satisfying. Mrs. Curran's account of the way in which her books were written is obviously based on very careful self-observation. She expressly states that although Patience Worth takes complete charge of her whilst writing is being done she, Mrs. Curran, remains in the background all the time. Her own comment on the partnership between them runs as follows: 'One of the most peculiar things about our work is that while I am writing there seems to be no definite place where *my* consciousness ceases and that of Patience Worth's comes in.' Now in all the well-known instances of multiple personality such as the well documented one of Sally Beauchamp, the different personalities within the person alternate with each other in their appearances and are never present at the same time. In many cases the different personalities are even ignorant of each other's existence. Consequently if we accept the split personality theory of Mrs. Curran's authorship we should have to regard Patience Worth as being a *supplementary*, or secondary, character rather than one of several co-equal personalities who made up Mrs. Curran. But before the source of Mrs. Curran's knowledge can be discussed with any profit, another remarkable case of automatic writing must be quoted.

The Willett Scripts

Astonishing though the writings of Mrs. Curran are, they are less remarkable than those produced by Mrs. Willett. Soon after the Society of Psychical Research had been founded Mrs. Willett took a leading part in some very well organized experiments on the phenomenon of automatic writing. 'Mrs. Willett' was the pseudonym adopted by a Mrs. Coombe-Tennant in order to hide her real identity during her own lifetime. In spite of the eminence of the founders of the S.P.R. and of the conscientiousness with which they were carrying out their investigations, anybody engaged at that time in psychical research was liable to be regarded as being 'queer'. For this reason Mrs. Coombe-Tennant preferred that the scripts, for which she was mainly responsible, should not be published under her real name. Mrs. Coombe-Tennant has now been dead for several years but her automatic writings still remain unpublished. This is unfortunate, for it was the unpublished parts of her script which made so deep an impression on the late Lord Balfour.

The 'Willett Writings' are remarkable for several reasons, the first being that 'Mrs. Willett' was a very highly educated and intelligent woman in a position to express her own views about the messages which were rising into her consciousness from the place of their origin, the Subliminal regions of her mind. The second reason for regarding Mrs. Willett's automatic writings as of exceptional interest is that she and her colleagues in the S.P.R. were convinced that the dead, as well as the living members of the S.P.R. were taking part in their production. Mrs. Willett herself had no doubt that the following four deceased member of the S.P.R. were collaborating with the living members of it; the psychologist, W. H. Myers, Professor Henry Sidgewick, Dr. Verrall and, at a somewhat later date, Henry Butcher, Professor of Greek at Edinburgh University. What supported her view was the fact that the contributions made by the deceased members of the party were said to be characterized by the same personal traits and idiosyncracies which had distinguished them when they were living. For example, the Willett scripts are sprinkled with philosophical reflections which Mrs. Willett almost always misunderstood and whenever this happened Gurney displayed, as he had invariably displayed in life, an irresistible disposition to be humorous about it. Afterwards he would do his best to help Mrs. Willett out of her difficulties but usually she would interrupt him, as she had done previously, with such exclamations as the following: 'Don't go . . . I'll try again. He's telling L. something.' (Sir Oliver Lodge was often present in the flesh at the sittings.) '. . . Oh, I'm buzzing.'

The communicators of the messages – whoever they were and whether they were alive or dead – all seemed to be in agreement with regard to the nature of the human mind. They looked upon man's *psyche* as being of a hierarchical nature made up of several levels of being, a fact which explains the appearance in the scripts of such phrases as: 'He (that is to say Gurney) says there are ranges of varying depths . . . He says there are many gradations . . . an ascending scale . . .' Gurney referred also in the Willett writings to the different levels in the Subliminal self and said that it 'graded up to and merged into' what he called the 'transcendental self' or 'central Unity'.

Many of the messages reputed to have come from the deceased members of the S.P.R. were delivered vocally by Mrs. Willett, instead of having to be written down and, whilst commenting on this at a later date, Lord Balfour occasionally referred to Mrs. Willett's 'mediumship'. But his use of the term 'mediumship' is misleading, for Mrs. Willett did not behave as the ordinary medium behaves in a spiritualistic séance. She also denied the existence in her of 'controls', that is to say of intermediaries between herself and the disincarnated spirits said to be speaking through her. Nor did Mrs. Willett go into a state of semi-trance in the way that mediums usually do in a spiritualistic séance. A certain amount of mental dissociation probably took place in her and that was all. It would seem also that Mrs. Willett's dead collaborators regarded it as being a matter of great importance that she should never be allowed to disappear into a trance state, but that she should always remain, to some extent, aware of herself and of her surroundings. There is every evidence that they took great care of her throughout the whole series of experiments, treating her as a delicate and sensitive instrument which had to be handled skilfully and gently. Thus we have Gurney interjecting the following comment into the script: 'I can't do much here today; *she* needs solitude and rest and the life-confused and jarring element in which she has been breathing is a bar.' This was recognized by the living members of the team so the meeting was brought to a close and Mrs. Willett was told to rest. So also, at a session presided over by Sir Oliver Lodge, do we find Gurney expressing to the chairman his concern about Mrs. Willett's psychological state and about her ability to carry on her work. 'Lodge . . . did you notice just now that she was completely over the border, and that though in those instants things swept into her consciousness, she couldn't pass them back?' Five years later, a similar warning was issued to the effect that conditions were not satisfactory for work but on this occasion the warning was given to Mrs. Willett herself and not, as before, to the Chairman. 'Today one touch would draw you so deeply within our influence that you would be unable to record a carry back.'

It is obvious that all of Mrs. Willett's communicators, and particularly Myers the acknowledged expert in psychology, regarded it as being a matter of the very greatest importance that Mrs. Willett's ordinary 'self' should remain, to some extent, present. They believed that communication between the living and the dead was maintained by means of telepathic messages passing backwards and forwards between the two parties. This being so it was necessary that Mrs. Willett should remain in what can be described as being an intermediate position, somewhere between her rational and her intuitive faculties. As Myers put it, what had to be found was '. . . the line where the incarnate spirit is sufficiently over the border to be in a state to *reason* and yet sufficiently controlled by its own power, by its own subliminal self'.

It is disappointing that experiments which were carried out by such intelligent researchers as were those engaged in the production of the Willett scripts should have yielded so little information about the conditions of existence on what is usually called 'the other side'. Very rarely was this subject of the state of the dead experimenters mentioned and then only to be dismissed with the remark that there were insuperable difficulties to discussing it. Lord Balfour makes the following comment about the obstacles to any understanding being reached between the living and the dead. 'The suggestion seems to be that the subliminal self of the discarnate being uses categories which are beyond the reach of the incarnated mind, much as the categories employed by the human mind are beyond the comprehension of animals.' This does not necessarily imply that the dead have reached a much higher level of understanding, for it is evident from the script that the knowledge possessed by the discarnate communicators was itself very limited, a fact which they themselves were the first to admit. Thus we have Gurney interjecting the following remark during a session: 'You never seem to realize how little we know . . . Sometimes I know and can't get it through, but very often I don't *know.*' So also had Myers remarked on a previous occasion: 'Remember there is as much room for knowledge in some ways here as with you, and many mysteries remain mysteries only to be approached from other and higher standpoints. I am going to begin fresh experiments and you might tell Mrs. Verrall when the opportunity occurs, that the need for experiments from this side has not been sufficiently grasped.'

The Willett scripts will be interpreted by different people in different ways and in accordance with individual philosophies and religious beliefs. There is much in these writings which cannot be explained satisfactorily along the psychological lines laid down in the first chapter of this book, namely the idea that there exists a subliminal self which is the source of much of our knowledge. So also is there a very marked difference between the automatic writings of Mrs. Willett and the statements usually made by professional mediums, a difference which can, to some extent, be accounted for by the superior intelligence and education of Mrs. Willett.

Perhaps the best way of assisting readers to reach a conclusion on this difficult subject is to start by giving them the opinion of Lord Balfour who was closely associated with the Willett experiments. Not only was he a man of great experience and sound judgement but he had been present at most of the sessions and had observed Mrs. Willett in action very carefully. His comments on the Willett script are as follows: 'If I had before me only those Willett scripts to which I have been referring, I frankly admit that I should have been at a loss whether to attribute them to subliminal activity or to a source entirely outside the personality of the medium. Probably, like Dr. Walter Prince, I should be content to suspend judgement. But having before me the *whole* of the Willett scripts and being in a position to compare them with the scripts of other automatists of our group and with facts known to me, but not known to Mrs. Willett herself, I am personally of the opinion that they contain evidence of super-normally acquired knowledge, which no mere subliminal mentations will suffice to account for.'[1]

Mrs. Sidgewick, the wife of Henry Sidgewick, was also a woman of very sound judgement and, like Lord Balfour, she was present at many of the Willett experiments. The conclusions she reached were similar to those expressed by her brother. In a speech made in 1913, she said: 'I should like to conclude by saying that, though we are not yet justified in feeling any certainty, I myself think that the evidence is pointing towards the conclusion that our fellow workers are still working with us.'[2]

We, who have access only to a portion of Mrs. Willett's writings possess insufficient information to allow of our arriving at any final decisions with regard

[1] Quoted by G. N. M. Tyrell, *Personality of Man.*
[2] idem.

to them. The question which concerns us most is whether the Willett experiments prove or do not prove the existence of discarnate minds. The author of this book confesses that he has a strong distaste for the explanations offered by the spiritualists and that he would prefer not to have recourse to them, but he admits that it is difficult to find a satisfactory alternative theory. If we are to avoid making use of a spiritualistic explanation we have to make two assumptions, first that Mrs. Willett possessed great skill in reproducing the mannerisms and the modes of thought of the deceased members of the S.P.R. and second, that she was able to obtain a great deal of information tele-pathetically from the minds of living people. Mrs. Willett herself was convinced that she obtained her knowledge from the discarnate spirits of the dead members of the S.P.R. and, in the end, Lord Balfour came to a similar conclusion. At a later date, G. N. M. Tyrell, a president of the S.P.R., reopened the whole question of the Willett scripts and he likewise was unable to find any method of accounting for them, other than the one favoured by Mrs. Willett herself. He summarized his conclusions as follows: 'It comes to this, that the phenomena of psychical research points strongly towards communications from the dead. It is possible to escape from this conclusion but only at the expense of introducing a still more extravagant hypothesis. The facts are quite clear. They cannot be got rid of by maintaining a masterly silence, by looking in the opposite direction or by making false statements about them. Sooner or later they will have to be faced. Those who wish to know the truth about the nature of the human individual might as well face them now."

The reader has now been provided with all the information available at present and he will have to come to his own conclusion about the Willett scripts. Having read Lord Balfour's and G. N. M. Tyrell's comments on them, he may well decide that he has no alternative to that of accepting their view that the scripts contain evidence of supernormally acquired knowledge which no theory of subliminal activity can account for. But this does not of necessity mean that he is forced to accept in its entirety a spiritualistic explanation of the Willett communications. The statement made by Lord Balfour was only to the effect that the scripts contained evidence of *supernormal mentations* which could not be entirely explained in terms of the subliminal self.

Belief in the existence of discarnate spirits entails belief also in the survival of the personality after the death of the body. As will be seen later I find it difficult to accept the idea of a personal form of survival and, this being so, I find it equally difficult to subscribe to the view that Mrs. Curran and Mrs. Willett obtained their knowledge from discarnate spirits. I prefer the idea that our minds are less well insulated from other systems of thought than we believe them to be and that mind-substance and mind-energy is to be found everywhere in the universe, just as matter and other forms of energy are to be found everywhere in the universe. This is one of the principles enunciated by the ancient science of Raja Yoga. This teaches that: 'Just as the Matter of which our physical bodies are

[1] G. N. M. Tyrell, *The Personality of Man.*

composed is really in touch with *all Matter* . . . so is our Mind-substance really in touch with all Mind-substance It is as if the "Ego" in its progress were moving through great oceans of Matter, Energy and Mind-substance. making use of that of each which is needed, and which immediately surrounds it, and leaving each behind as it moves on through the great volume of the ocean . . . This may bring more clearly before your mind the great Unity of things – may enable you to see things as a Whole, rather than as separate parts.' So wrote that notable exponent of Raja Yoga, Sri Ramacharaka.[1]

But quite apart from what ancient Hindu teaching has to tell us, the Western psychologists are now approaching a similar conclusion, that individual minds are not so clearly separated from one another, and are not so encapsulated and insulated from each other as they were formerly thought to be. This idea is finding expression in many different ways and, amongst others, in Jung's theory of a 'Collective Unconscious'. Personally I regard Jung's term 'Collective Unconscious' as being a little confusing because it tends to perpetuate the error which Western psychologists have frequently made, the error of failing to differentiate between the two entirely different concepts of 'consciousness' and 'function'. Consciousness is not a function but is an awareness of a function, that is to say an awareness of such activities as thinking, feeling and moving. But when Jung is talking about the Collective

[1] Yogi Ramacharaka, *Rajah Yoga*, L. N. Fowler & Co., London, 1917. (It should be noted that Ramacharaka uses the word 'Ego' in a different sense to that in which the author of this book uses it. For him the 'Ego' is not the *persona* or egotistical element in a man but the *Atman* or spiritual element in him.)

Unconscious he is not so much referring to a state of unconsciousness or total unawareness as to a collection of archetypal ideas and symbols common to us all. In other words, he is supporting the idea that our minds are not so completely insulated from other minds as we have imagined them to be and that at times we may be capable of extracting new ideas and knowledge from our environment.

This is no new idea. In the twelfth century a philosopher was born who taught that the ideas reached by our intellects are not necessarily our own ideas but that they may be common to the whole of humanity. Averroes was a Moslem philosopher who, during the Moslem occupation of Spain, was exiled by the Caliph for heresy to a small village near Cordoba. He was a follower of Aristotle and he taught that whilst we undoubtedly have separate bodies, we do not necessarily possess separate minds. Another way of putting this would be to say that we are all immersed in Universal Mind and that we derive from this common source similar, if not identical ideas. The organ by means of which the individual takes in mental nutriment from his surroundings is his brain and although at death he loses this contact with universal mind and disappears, Universal Mind still goes on. There is a marked similarity between the philosophy of Averroes, the Moor, and the teaching of Raja Yoga. The latter proclaims that during man's lifetime his 'ego' or 'personality' moves through an uncharted ocean of Matter, Energy and Mind, absorbing from it whatever it requires for its own sustenance. It is a theory for which a great deal of support can be found.

3

Telepathy

In all probability man has always believed that thoughts could sometimes be transmitted from one mind to another mind *directly* and not through the usual channels of the special senses. This belief is as widespread as it is ancient, and it is particularly prevalent in primitive communities. Telepathy, as this direct transmission of thought has been called, may take place in a variety of ways, and under many different conditions. Sometimes the *recipient* of the message has been widely awake, sometimes he has been in a drowsy condition, and sometimes he has received the message in the form of a dream. So also have the circumstances of the *sender* of the message differed. Frequently he has been in a highly critical situation, so that the message has been accepted by the recipient as a warning of his death, but on other occasions nothing of any consequence is happening either to the recipient or the transmitter of the message. Telepathy may therefore take place under so many different conditions that it is likely to be occurring sometimes without our being aware of the fact.

Many instances of telepathy are to be found in the Old Testament and in classical literature. There is the biblical story of the accusation brought against the prophet Elisha, to the effect that he was responsible for the leakage of news from the secret Council Chamber of the King of Syria. The King had discovered the

existence of this leakage and he complained of it to his
Councillors in the following words: 'Will you not show
me which of us is for the King of Israel?' To this they
answered 'None, my Lord O King, Elisha, the prophet
that is in Israel, telleth the King of Israel the words
thou speakest in thy bedchamber'.

So also is there the classical story of the special test
to which Croesus submitted the Oracle of Delphi in
order to find out whether it were true that she possessed
the capacity to know what was happening anywhere in
Greece. Heroditus narrates that the King's emissary,
dispatched to Delphi, was instructed to put to the
Oracle at a certain hour the following question:
'What is King Croesus, son of Alyaltes doing at this
very moment?' and the Oracle answered without any
hesitation that she could smell the savoury odour of
cooking and that lamb and tortoise were being roasted
together in the same dish. This answer was perfectly
correct, for Croesus had arranged to be engaged in the
most unlikely task possible, and to be cooking a highly
unusual dish at the time that his emissary was putting
the test question to the Oracle of Delphi.

St. Augustine also recounts in his writings how one
of his own disciples requested Albicarius, a Carthaginian
diviner, to reveal his, the questioner's, particular
thoughts at that moment and he states that Albicarius
not only answered him correctly but even recited to
him the passage in Virgil which was running through
his head. There can be no doubt that the phenomenon
of thought transference was widely accepted in Ancient
Greece, for Democritus not only refers to it but ventures
even to put forward a theory as to how telepathy

worked. But the leaders of the early Christian Church discouraged such ideas and practices, for they were of the opinion that they were likely to lead to deception and fraud. This being so, the Church placed a ban not only on telepathy but on all forms of psychical research. Not that the ban prevented people from investigating interesting phenomena of this kind. All that the Church's edict achieved was to compel those who were interested in them to carry out their researches in secret or behind some such *façade* as the study of chemistry. Many remarkable lines of research were pursued in this way by the Alchemists, the Rosicrucians and the Neo-Platonists. But psychic investigation remained all this time in the hands only of individuals and, as has been pointed out, it was not until the close of the nineteenth century that a special society was organized in order to carry on research on a larger scale. Even then the investigation of telepathy or thought-transmission continued to meet with considerable opposition, not so much from the Church as from the scientists.

Research on Telepathy

The Society for Psychical Research started a special investigation of telepathy and telepathic dreams very soon after its formation. Myers was responsible for replacing the older term 'thought-transference' by the new term 'telepathy' but in a way both words were inappropriate for they suggested that thought was actually being transported through space and, so far as can be ascertained, this is not the case. Previously, the phenomenon of telepathy fell under the general heading of *clairvoyance* or 'lucidite', a term which has the advantage that it offers no explanation of the way in which telepathy works.

The first step taken by the newly formed society was to submit accounts of spontaneous thought-transference to a very careful scrutiny and because two of the founding members, Myers and Gurney, were interested in spiritualism, telepathic warnings of illness or of death conveyed by dreams and by apparitions were included amongst the cases examined. At a later date accounts of these cases were published together in two books, entitled *Phantasms of the Living* and *Phantasms of the Dead*. It is to these books that I owe the examples of telepathic dreams and telepathic apparitions quoted in this chapter.

The first of these examples recounts how a ten-year-old girl was walking slowly and reluctantly towards her school, taking a final glance at her homework in geometry, and how suddenly her surroundings became dim to her and she had a vision of her mother lying prostrate on the floor of her bedroom in the home she had recently left. And on the floor near to her mother lay also a lace handkerchief. So convincing and so startling was this vision of her mother that the girl did not hesitate for a moment but ran straight to the house of the family doctor, living nearby, and persuaded him to return with her at once to her home. On arrival there the doctor found everything precisely as the child had reported it to be. The mother had apparently suffered from a heart attack and she was lying stretched out on the floor of the room in which the child had seen her, with a lace handkerchief beside her. It can, of course, be argued that the mother was subject to heart attacks, that the child had seen her in one of these before, that she had been a little bit nervous about her mother that very morning and that her imagination had created the whole scene. But there is nothing in the carefully written report of the incident which suggests that the doctor had previously treated her mother for heart trouble, and it is highly unlikely that the investigator who questioned the doctor failed to record a fact so important as that her mother had previously suffered from heart attacks.

The second case of spontaneous telepathy to be taken from *Phantasms of the Living* differs from the first case in that the recipient was asleep at the time that the message came to him, so that it was received by him in the form of a dream. The account is given in the first person.

'My brother and father were on a journey and I dreamt that I saw father driving in a sledge with one horse, followed by my brother in another sledge. They had to pass a crossroad on which another traveller was driving very fast, also in a sledge with one horse. Father seemed to drive on without observing the other fellow who would . . . have driven over Father if he had not made his horse rear, so that I saw Father drive under the hooves of the horse. Every moment I expected the horse to fall down and crush him. I called out "Father, Father . . ." and awoke in a fright.' Later it was found that everything that had happened occurred just as the percipient had described it.

Telepathy and Apparitions

At an early stage of their investigation, Myers and

Gurney found very close links between the two phenomena of 'telepathy' and 'apparitions' and this necessitated that they should extend the scope of their researches. After having examined a great many histories of apparitions they came to the conclusion that, contrary to popular belief, apparitions were not something occurring outside the observer in external space, but that they were the result of events occurring within him. They also believed that in many cases *two* people were responsible for the presence of an apparition, the first being the *agent* or distant person who started things going and the second the *percipient* or person who saw the apparition. In their opinion the apparition started as an hallucination in the less conscious regions of the percipient's mind and then rose up into the more conscious levels of it where it was given a form which these levels were able to accept. Myers and Gurney assumed that the two people responsible for the production of the apparition, the *agent* and the *percipient* were in touch with each other telepathetically. In order to illustrate how the two co-operated, Gurney quoted the following story, narrated in the first person by the percipient, a young woman called Frances Reddell.

'Helen Alexander (maid to Lady Waldegrave) was lying ill with typhoid fever, and she was attended by me. I was standing at the table by her bedside, pouring out her medicine, at about 4 o'clock in the morning of the 4th October 1880. I heard the call-bell ring (this had been heard twice before during the night in that same week), and I was attracted by the door of the room opening and by seeing a person entering the room whom I instantly felt to be the mother of the sick woman. She had a brass candlestick in her hand, a red shawl over her shoulders, and a flannel petticoat which had a hole in the front. I looked at her as much as to say: "I am glad you have come", but the woman looked at me sternly, as much as to say, "Why wasn't I sent for before?" I gave the medicine to Helen Alexander, and then turned round to speak to the vision, but no one was there. She had gone. She was a short, dark person and very stout. At about six o'clock that morning Helen Alexander died. Two days after, her parents and a sister came to Antony, and arrived between one and two o'clock in the morning; I and another maid let them in, and it gave me a great turn when I saw the living likeness of the vision I had seen two nights before. I told the sister about the vision, and she said that the description of the dress exactly answered to her mother's, and that they had brass candlesticks at home exactly like the one described. There was not the slightest resemblance between the mother and daughter. (Signed – Frances Reddell.)'

The above description of a ghostly visitor was given by Miss Reddell to her employer, Lady Waldegrave, a few hours after the apparition had occurred, so that the whole incident was fresh in her mind. Miss Reddell also prefaced her account with the following words: 'I am not superstitious or nervous, and I wasn't in the least frightened, but her mother came to see her last night.' It is difficult to dismiss the whole story as a phantasy in the mind of an overtired servant, or as a tale which she made up after meeting the dead girl's mother. What struck the members of the committee of the Society for Psychical Research responsible for the investigation of this case very forcibly was that Miss Reddell's description of the figure she had seen resembled so closely what would have been the appearance of the mother had she risen suddenly from bed in order that she might visit her sick daughter. Not only was the candlestick of the same pattern as those used in her house, but so also was there a hole in the front of Mrs. Alexander's petticoat, a hole produced by the way in which she was accustomed to wear that garment.

This story illustrates another point which the committee found to be true of the great majority of accounts of apparitions. It was that the mere fact that someone has suffered from an hallucination does not necessarily mean that he or she has an unbalanced mind. Many of the people who reported that they had experienced apparitions were quiet, matter-of-fact and responsible persons who had never experienced anything of a similar nature previously. The girl Reddell was regarded as being a reliable and trustworthy young woman by everybody who knew her. It should also be noted that the figure she had seen in the room was not a vague and nebulous one but a form so clearly outlined that she was able to describe both its facial expression and the small hole in the front of the petticoat. Although the hallucination resembled very closely what would have been seen had an old woman carrying a brass candlestick and wearing a red shawl actually entered the room, the modes of perception in the two were entirely different. The spectacle of a flesh and blood woman would have been the result of stimulation of the percipient's retina followed by the passage of sensory messages up to the visual centre in the brain, whereas an hallucination would be likely to have arisen from a *direct* excitation of the visual centre in the brain. In other words, apparitions arise in the same way that remembered images, imagined figures and dream-figures arise, by a direct excitation of the visual centre in the brain.

The condition which is likely to be favourable to the production of an hallucination is a slight lowering of the level of consciousness in the percipient, but a lowering insufficient to induce actual sleep, whereas the visualizing carried out deliberately by artists demands the careful focusing of their attention on to what they wish to create. It will be noted that the figure in the red shawl made no demands at all on Miss Reddell's attention but that it formed itself spontaneously, and without any effort on her part, whilst she was occupied with something else, namely with thinking about the dose of medicine which had to be administered to her patient. Myers explains Miss Reddell's projection into the room of the apparition of a stout old woman, dressed in a flannel petticoat, in the following way: 'Now what I imagine to have happened is this. The mother, anxious about her daughter, paid her a "psychical visit" during the sleep of both. In so doing she actually modified a certain portion of space, not materially or optically, but in such a manner that persons, perceptive in a certain fashion, would discern in that part of space an image approximately corresponding to the conception of her own aspect, latent in the invading mother's mind. A person thus susceptible happened to be in the room, and thus, as a bystander, witnessed a psychical invasion whose memory the invader (the mother) apparently did not retain, whilst the invaded person – the due percipient (the sick daughter) – may or may not have perceived it in a dream, but died and left no sign of having done so.'

Myers's explanation of what happened is not very satisfactory, for he is making a great number of assumptions, such as the assumption that Helen Alexander's mother was anxious about her daughter and that she paid Miss Reddell a 'psychical visit'. But what does he mean by the term 'psychical visit'? Later in his report he substitutes for 'psychical visit' the new term 'psychical invasion' without commenting on it. Is he referring to the ancient idea of invasion or possession by a 'spirit', the idea that an individual's personality may be temporarily displaced by the intrusion of the personality of somebody else, so that the latter takes over the control of the invaded person's body and brain? In all probability he meant something a little less radical than this but of the same general nature.

Some indication of what was in Myers's mind when he made the above comment on the mode of production of Miss Reddell's hallucination may be inferred from his account of an hallucination which was deliberately planned. In *Human Personality* Myers points out that two people are usually responsible for the production of an apparition, namely the *percipient* and the *agent*. In order to illustrate the dual nature of many apparitions and the parts which are played in their production by the agent and the percipient he recounts the story of a young man, S. H. B., who deliberately planned an experiment in apparition production. S. H. B. tells his story in the first person.

'On a certain Sunday evening in November 1881, having been reading of the great power which the human will is capable of exercising, I determined, with the whole force of my being, that I would be present in spirit in the front bedroom on the second floor of a house situated at 22 Hogarth Road, Kensington, in which room slept two ladies of my acquaintance, viz., Miss L. S. V. and Miss E. C. V. aged respectively twenty-five and eleven years. I was living at this time at 23 Kildare Gardens, a distance of about three miles from Hogarth Road, and I had not mentioned, in any way, my intention of trying an experiment to either of the above ladies, for the simple reason that it was only on retiring to rest upon this Sunday night that I made up my mind to do this. The time at which I determined I would be there at 22 Hogarth Road was one o'clock in the morning, and I also had a strong intention of making my presence perceptible.

'On the following Thursday, I went to see the ladies in question and in the course of conversation (without any allusion to the subject on my part) the elder one told me that on the previous Sunday night she had been much terrified by perceiving me standing by her bedside and that she screamed when the apparition advanced towards her, and awoke her little sister, who saw me also.

'I asked her if she was awake at the time and she replied most decidedly in the affirmative and, upon my inquiring the time of the occurrence she replied, about one o'clock in the morning.

'This lady, at my request, wrote down a statement of the event and signed it.

'This was the first occasion upon which I tried an experiment of this kind and its complete success startled me very much.

'Besides exercising my power of volition very strongly, I had put forth an effort which I cannot find words to describe. I was conscious of a mysterious influence of some sort permeating in my body and had a distinct impression that I was exercising some force with which I had been hitherto unacquainted, but which I can now at certain times set in motion at will. (S. H. B.)'

Of the original entry in the almanac diary, S. H. B. says: 'I recollect having made it within a week or so of the occurrence of the experiment and whilst it was perfectly fresh in my memory.'

Miss Verity's account of the incident is as follows: 'January 19th, 1883. On a certain Sunday evening about twelve months since, at our house in Hogarth Road, Kensington, I distinctly saw Mr. B. in my room, about one o'clock. I was perfectly awake and was much terrified. I awoke my sister by screaming and she saw the apparition herself. Three days after, when I saw Mr. B., I told him what had happened, but it was some time before I could recover from the shock I had received; and the remembrance is too vivid to be ever erased from my memory. (L. S. Verity.)'

In answer to inquiries, Miss Verity adds: 'I had never had any hallucinations of the senses of any sort whatever.'

Miss E. C. Verity says:

'I remember the occurrence of the event described by

my sister in the annexed paragraph and her description is quite correct. I saw the apparition which she saw at the same time and under the same circumstances. (E. C. Verity.)'

Miss A. S. Verity says:

'I remember quite clearly the evening my elder sister awoke me by calling to me from an adjoining room; and upon my going to her bedside where she slept with my youngest sister, they both told me that they had seen S. H. B. standing in the room. The time was about one o'clock. S. H. B. was in evening dress they told me. (A. S. Verity.)'

Mr. S. H. B. does not remember how he was dressed on the night of the occurrence.

Miss E. C. Verity was asleep when her sister caught sight of the figure and was awoken by her sister's exclaiming 'There is S.' The name had therefore met her ear before she herself saw the figure; and the hallucination on her part might therefore be attributed to suggestion. But it is against this view that she has never had any other hallucination and cannot therefore be considered as predisposed to such experiences. The sisters are both equally certain that the figure was in evening dress and that it stood in one particular spot in the room. The gas was burning low and the phantasmal figure was seen with far more clearness than a real form would have been.

'The witnesses (says Gurney) have been very carefully cross-examined by the present writer. There is not the slightest doubt that their mention of the occurrence to S. H. B. was spontaneous. They had not at first intended to mention it but when they saw him their sense of its oddness overcame their resolution. Miss Verity is a perfectly sober-minded and sensible witness, with no love of marvels, and with a considerable dread and dislike of this particular form of marvel.'

A special committee of the S.P.R. interrogated the two Miss V.s as well as the third sister who had been sleeping in an adjoining room. The two sisters, L. S. V. and E. C. V. confirmed that they had seen an apparition of S. H. B. at one o'clock in the morning, and the third sister, A. S. V., stated that she had been summoned specially into her sisters' room that night in order to be told about what had happened. At the request of the committee the experiment was repeated by S. H. B. and apparently with similar success.

The Limitations of the Method of Investigating Telepathy by the Examination of Spontaneous Cases

Many well-attested accounts of telepathic and prophetic dreams were collected by the S.P.R. So also did the society examine reports of cases in which one person became suddenly aware of what was happening to someone else in a distant town, but the limitations of these methods of research were soon revealed. The members of the examining committee were always left with a number of questions which could not be satisfactorily answered. How much had the narrator added to his account of his telepathic dream *after* the details of the event he had dreamed of had been revealed to him? The temptation to make his story more convincing by means of these later additions would undoubtedly be a very compelling one. How trustworthy were the various witnesses and how much of

the story could be accounted for by chance? Strange
coincidences happened from time to time and they
might easily be mistaken for examples of telepathy.
And even if the account of the telepathic incident
was a trustworthy one, might not what had
happened be equally well accounted for by clairvoyance? Spontaneous cases of telepathy such as those
investigated by the committee contained too many
unknown quantities to be satisfactory material for
research. After examining a very large number of
cases with the greatest care, the committee was able to
discover very little about the nature of the phenomenon
it was studying. In view of their poor results it
was decided that if progress was to be made a much
more exact method of studying telepathy must be
devised.

This does not mean that nothing had been learnt
from the careful study of spontaneous cases of telepathy.
The committee had learnt a great deal from this study
and it was now of the opinion that telepathy was a
genuine phenomenon and, like clairvoyance, a function
of the Subliminal regions of the mind. In some manner
or other a message passed at the subliminal level
between two minds, and then, having reached its
destination, rose up into the more conscious levels of
the *percipient's* mind so that he became aware of it.
The earlier workers on telepathy assumed that telepathic messages travelled across physical space in the
form of thought-radiations, an idea which received
strong support when wireless was discovered. So
satisfied were these earlier workers with this radiation
explanation of telepathy that Dr. Ivor Lloyd Tucker, a

Fellow of Trinity College, Cambridge, remarked that 'belief in telepathy meant nothing more than believing in the existence of vibrations in the ether, resulting from and acting on nervous matter'.[1]

Further thought revealed many objections to this over-simplified view of telepathy. Not only was there no evidence in favour of the passage of radiations across space but there were several serious objections to this idea. If telepathy were of a similar nature to wireless the brain of the sender would have to be equipped with some form of transmitter, and a transmitter of considerable power when the agent and the recipient were separated by great distances from each other, and no organs remotely resembling a transmitter and a receiving organ had been discovered by the anatomists and the physiologists. It was true that electric waves passed over the surface of the brain whenever it became active but these waves were too weak to be capable of travelling across miles of physical space. Another argument against the radiation theory of telepathy was that all physical radiations obey what is known as the 'inverse square law', that is to say, the law which proclaims that their intensity varies inversely with the square of the distance from their source. This law is very obvious in the case of light, but there is not, and never has been, any evidence that telepathy conforms to it. It appears to be just as easy, or just as difficult, as the case may be, to transmit a telepathic message into the adjoining room as it is to project it across the Atlantic. A final and still greater objection to the physical radiation theory is that in

[1] Quoted by G. N. M. Tyrell in *The Personality of Man.*

order to send verbal messages by physical signalling, a code must first be agreed upon by the parties concerned, for unless the receiver of the message is aware of the nature of this code, the physical signals he has received will be entirely meaningless to him. All of these considerations made it unlikely, from the very start, that telepathy would ever be explained in terms of physical radiations.

Carrington's Association Theory of Telepathy

Whateley Carrington has put forward for consideration a theory now known as Carrington's Association Theory of Telepathy. Experience shows us that words and ideas often hunt in couples so that if one word or idea comes into the mind it is likely to be followed by some associated word or idea. For example, the giant Magog follows close on the heels of his companion giant Gog, and Swan cannot be mentioned without his partner, Edgar, quickly appearing. If someone speaks to me of a railway, the word Southern immediately comes into my mind and I have fleeting pictures of platforms, signals and over-crowded carriages. But what bearing has all this on the phenomenon of telepathy? Whateley Carrington introduces his Association Theory in connexion with certain experiments he made on telepathy. These experiments consisted of hanging up every night in his study one of a series of drawings he had previously made and by inviting a number of people living at different distances from his house to state what was the subject of that particular night. He was of the opinion that the successes scored in this test were greater than could be accounted for by chance and he attempted to account for these successes by means of his association theory. He writes as follows on this subject. 'Consider one of my experiments with drawings. In my capacity of experimenter, I sit down at my desk and my first step is to decide on what I shall draw as an Original by opening a dictionary at random. Let us give the name "O" to the object which I thus decide on drawing; the reader can substitute for this any particular object such as House, Jug, Ship, etc. I accordingly set to work to draw "O". This inevitably means that at least some of the various images which make up my idea of "O" will be present in my mind in greater or lesser degree. But so also will many other ideas, including sensations derived from my surroundings . . . Suppose that before I started I placed on my desk some special and rather unusual object, not ordinarily there, K . . . Then my field of consciousness as I work will include . . . sensations or percepts occasioned by the presence of the object K; and the idea will become associated with, amongst other things, the idea X . . . But if *you* are a *subject* working in the experiment the sight of K on *your* desk would not tend to draw up the idea of O from your subconscious and you would be no more likely to think of O than if K were *not* there; and the fact that K and O were associated in *my* subconscious would have nothing to do with it. Why? Because we always take it for granted that *your* subconscious and *mine* are *separate*. *But suppose they are not separate.* Suppose we have a common subconscious. Suppose we can draw on a common repository . . . then the presentation of K to you *will* tend to draw up the idea O and you *will* be more likely to think of O . . . And you will tend to draw the same things that I do.'

Whateley Carrington next asks the question 'What is it that acts as the K object in these experiments and draws *agent* and *percipient* together?' His answer is that the connecting link between the *agent* and the *percipient* is the *idea* of the experiment. It is the presence of this common fact that both are taking part in the same experiment which makes the experiments devised by Carrington an entirely different matter from two people idly doodling on different bits of paper.

The Idea that Individual Minds are not entirely Separate Entities

Carrington's Association Theory has certain advantages over both the wireless theory of telepathy and what may be called the 'sixth sense' view of it. It does not require of us that we should postulate the existence in the human body of a hitherto undiscovered transmitting and receiving set and it eliminates all need for a preliminary tuning in, and for a subsequent decoding of the signals received. The only form of machinery it demands is the well-known mechanism of word and idea association. It does however require something of ourselves. It requires of us that we should put aside, for the time being, the assumption we have always made that minds are separate and private entities and this is a concession which may not be an easy one for us to make. Our mannerisms of thought are as deeply ingrained in us as are our individual methods of moving and of feeling and we may well reject, at sight, this highly novel conception that our minds are less our own than we have always imagined them to be. Actually Carrington's idea of a linkage between the unconscious regions of various minds is neither illogical nor entirely novel.

Another philosophical difficulty remains to be dealt with, a difficulty which has been aggravated by the fact that in previous discussions on the subject of telepathy use has been made of words coined for the special purpose of describing the movement of physical objects in space. For example, the statement has been made about an idea being 'transmitted' from one mind to another mind and about the distance between two minds making little difference and such talk as this is misleading. When we describe Mr. X as 'passing' from a state of calm into one of intense fear, we are not tricked into believing that a movement in space has actually occurred, but in discussing telepathy we are all liable to forget that the words we use to indicate movement are used only metaphorically. The risk of our forgetting this is increased by our tendency to equate the two words 'mind' and 'brain'. Now it is quite true that the *brains* of A and B occupy two different positions in physical space but this does not necessarily mean that the *minds* of A and B also occupy different areas of space. *Physical* space is a concept which should be kept for use with *physical* entities, made of ordinary forms of matter, for space unoccupied by matter has as little meaning as has matter unpossessed of space.

The last philosophical question requiring consideration is the question whether an idea can ever be considered to be a *material* entity and, as such, entitled to be given a position in physical space. The answer to this question will depend entirely on the philosophy of the person seeking an answer to it. The great majority of the readers of this book are likely to be dualists who have accepted without question Descartes's sharp division between a material body and an ·immaterial mind. For such dualistic thinkers an idea can never be said to stand in a relationship with physical space. So also is the idealist debarred from thinking of mind as being situated anywhere in physical space. It is only the materialist of that peculiar breed to which the author of this book happens to belong and the 'neutral monist' of the Bertrand Russell variety, in other words a philosopher who looks upon mind and matter as being different aspects of a single and anterior entity, who are entitled to think of minds as being situated in different areas of physical space. This subject is a highly technical one and it will be discussed at greater length in the later chapters of this book.

4

The Scientific Investigation of Telepathy

Science is based on observation and experiment and the scientific investigation of telepathy may be said to have started, very modestly, with 'parlour games' carried out by intelligent amateurs. Professor Gilbert Murray and his family were amongst the earlier pioneers in this field of scientific research. Between 1910 and 1915, the professor and his daughter, Mrs. Arnold Toynbee, carried out a number of home experiments, the results of which were afterwards published in the Proceedings of the S.P.R. The method employed was a very simple one. Gilbert Murray retired whilst the experimenters were choosing a suitable subject, which was duly noted down on paper, as was also every remark made by Gilbert Murray on being readmitted to the room. The results of his guesses, without any questioning on the part of the others, were assessed as follows: Successes, 33 per cent; partial successes, 27.9 per cent; failures, 39 per cent. Professor Murray makes the following comments on these results: 'But it may be remarked that as evidence for the presence of some degree of telepathy most of the partial successes are quite as convincing as the complete successes; this would produce something like 60 per cent evidential and 40 per cent non-evidential.'

Professor Murray's description of his state of mind whilst trying to name the chosen subject is of particular interest. He writes:

'Of course, the personal impression of the percipient himself is by no means conclusive evidence but I do feel there is one almost universal quality in these guesses of mine which does suit telepathy and does not suit any other explanation. They always begin with a vague emotional quality or atmosphere: "This is horrible; this is grotesque; this is full of anxiety;" or rarely: "This is something delightful;" or sometime: "This is out of a book; this is a Russian novel" or the like. That seems like a direct impression of some human mind. Even in the failures, this feeling of atmosphere often gets through. That is, it was not so much an act of cognition, or a piece of information that was transferred to me, but rather a feeling of an emotion; and it is notable that I never had any success in guessing mere cards or numbers, or any subject that was not in some way interesting or amusing.'

It is clear from what Professor Murray says here that a person who is endeavouring to receive a telepathic message is more likely to receive the message in an emotional than in an intellectual form. In other words, he *feels* rather than *thinks* it, and because our emotional functions are more easily disturbed than are our intellectual functions it is not in the least surprising that emotional upsets often interfere with telepathic receptivity. Professor Murray gives us a description of the state of mind which he believes to be favourable to obtaining positive results. He writes: 'The conditions which suited me best were in many ways much the same as those which professional mediums have some-times insisted on. This is suspicious, yet fraud, I think, is out of the question; however slippery the behaviour of my subconscious, too many respectable people would have had to be its accomplices. I liked the general atmosphere to be friendly and familiar; any feeling of ill-temper or hostility was apt to spoil the experiment. Noises or interruptions had a bad effect.'

In the earlier days of parapsychological research it was recognized that a state of partial dissociation was a favourable one, and the subjects of the earliest experiments of all were usually hypnotized prior to the telepathic experiments being carried out on them. Mesmer set this fashion and he describes how one of his patients succeeded in discovering the whereabouts of a lost dog by these means. Mesmer induced in her what he called 'a state of somnambulism' and then, whilst in this condition, she gave instructions to her maid to fetch a gendarme. When the latter arrived she ordered him to go to a certain street, about a quarter of a mile distant, where he would meet a woman carrying a dog. She instructed him to stop this woman and to take possession of the dog which did not really belong to her. Everything happened in accordance with the orders the gendarme had received and Mesmer's patient recovered her lost pet. So also did the French psychologist Richet experiment with subjects whom he had previously hypnotized. He claimed that whilst in this state they were often able to identify playing cards enclosed within opaque envelopes.

But gradually telepathy and clairvoyance were freed from their association with hypnosis and were studied in subjects in an ordinary psychological state. A number of different tests devised for this purpose were employed, a favourite one being to ask the subject to describe, or to make a rough drawing of, some object which had been previously chosen by the agent or experimenter. The majority of those who conducted these tests were fully convinced that the results which they had obtained could not possibly be attributed to accident. Many variations were made, both in the techniques employed and in the type of subject chosen, and the most outstanding results I have been able to find are those which were recorded in 1935 by Professor Ferdinand von Neureiter of Riga. An account of his experiments is given by Dr. Jan Ehrenweld in his excellent little book *Telepathy and Medical Psychology*. Professor Neureiter was fortunate enough to discover an exceptionally brilliant subject for his experiments, a nine-year-old Lithuanian girl, whom he calls Ilga K. Although she had been an ordinary baby at birth and had developed in other respects satisfactorily, she was extremely backward so far as speaking and reading were concerned. In her reading she never managed to progress beyond the stage of recognizing the letters of the alphabet. Then her school teacher accidentally discovered that, although Ilga had these marked disabilities, she was able to read from a book if he, or someone else, happened to be standing near to her and were to read a passage silently to himself or even if he were only to *think* the passage. In these special circumstances, Ilga was able to read to him what she had never managed to read before. 'In fact she could read any context required, in any foreign language, although she had command of the Lithuanian language only.' But it was always necessary that somebody else should *think* the passage first. Only then did it become possible for Ilga to read it.

In most of the experiments described by Neureiter he acted as the *agent* but sometimes the part of the *agent* was played either by a colleague of his or else by the child's mother or her elder brother, aged eleven. Usually Ilga and the agent were placed in separate rooms but occasionally they sat in the same room with their backs turned towards each other, and usually with a curtain in between them. Special precautions were taken to avoid any unconscious whispering or gestures. In one of the experiments, Neureiter wrote down on a sheet of paper: $4.4 \times 5.5 = 41$ and he then handed the paper to Ilga's mother, who was acting on this occasion as agent. Her mother turned towards him complaining that she did not understand what had been written on the paper and the professor was just about to explain to her what the dots meant when Ilga suddenly, and quite unexpectedly, uttered the number 41. 'Obviously her mother, following Professor Neureiter's explanation, was just considering the result of the calculation and at that moment the "transmitting" took place.'

In another of the experiments a list of words and figures was handed to Ilga's mother, who was seated behind a curtain, whilst Ilga herself was playing about in front of it under the observation of the experimenters. Without interrupting her game or waiting to be told to do this, Ilga repeated without any fault, the whole list of words and figures which had been given to her mother: *ger*, *til*, *tli*, 123, 213, 312. Neureiter states that on such occasions as these Ilga's voice was different from her ordinary speaking voice, each of the syllables being pronounced by her in a stilted manner. Ilga was much more successful when her mother acted as agent than with anybody else. On one occasion, Ilga's mother mistook a figure on the list which had been given to her and Ilga repeated her mother's mistake, thus indicating that although the compiler of the list may have had in his mind what he had written on the paper, the part of agent was always played by her mother.

Ilga was submitted to an intelligence test and she attained only the standard of a child of four. Her most pronounced disability was in reading in the ordinary way and all that she ever managed to do was to recognize some of the letters. She remained incapable of reading even the shortest word. All this strongly suggests that Ilga suffered from what is known as congenital 'word blindness' or *alexia*. There exist separate centres in the brain for the *reading* of words and for the understanding of *spoken* words. and it was the former word-seeing centre which was so deficient in Ilga. Yet she was able to reproduce without error long passages read by her mother in an adjoining room, even when they were read in German, French, English or Latin.

Whateley Carrington's Experiments in Telepathy

Experiments in telepathy were also carried out in London by Mr. Whateley Carrington. He reduced them to the simplest possible form. At about 7 o'clock on ten successive evenings one of a series of ten drawings previously made was pinned up in his study. The objects selected for drawing had been picked at random out of a dictionary. The door of Carrington's study was locked and the selected drawings remained there until the next morning, nobody except Carrington and his wife being aware of the subject for that evening. Carrington had previously made arrangements with no less than 251 *percipients*, all of whom lived at a considerable distance from the place in which the drawings were being displayed. They had been asked to make a drawing every evening of what they believed would be on display on that particular night in Carrington's study. The percipient's drawings were then sent to certain independent judges for assessment and this was naturally by far the most difficult part of the experiment. Professors C. D. Broad and H. H. Price and Dr. R. H. Thouless acted as assessors and in their opinion the percipients scored many more hits than could be accounted for by accident alone. Another interesting and unexpected fact derived from their examination of the drawing was that hits were frequently made, not on the actual night of the test but, on the drawings which were displayed on the *previous* and on the *subsequent* nights, or even on the drawings shown *two nights before* or *two nights after* the target night. For example, if the drawing of a bird had been hung up in Carrington's study on, say a Tuesday evening, percipients were liable to draw an object resembling a bird, not only on that particular evening but on the evenings immediately preceding it or following it. In other words, there was a time displacement which might be either forwards or backwards. As the result of this displacement the scoring card took on the 'scatter' appearance to be seen on a target around the central bull's eye, but in this case it was a 'scatter' in *time* and not in *space*.

This method of testing the capacity of various subjects for telepathy constituted a great advance on the older method of examining only spontaneous cases of telepathy. But it could not be considered ideal, for whilst it was true that the agent had chosen the subject for transmission at hazard out of a dictionary opened accidentally there was no guarantee that a leakage of information had not occurred subsequently, in some roundabout way. However striking the results might be to those who were actually engaged in the test, they would never convince other people until some means were found of determining to what extent chance was responsible for the positive results obtained. Credit must be given to Dr. J. B. Rhine of Duke University for supplying what was needed and for thus remedying these defects. Although he was not the first person to employ card-guessing tests in telepathy, his carefully controlled work at Duke University can be said to have started a new era in the history of parapsychological research.

The Quantitative Tests carried out at Duke University, North Carolina

Dr. Rhine began by devising a number of card-guessing tests to which he afterwards submitted student volunteers. Never before had cards been employed for this purpose on so large a scale. A much simplified pack was designed for general use, a pack consisting of twenty-five cards bearing the following five symbols; a star, rectangle, cross, circle and wavy lines. There were five cards of each design and the pack became known as the ESP or Zener pack of cards. At the start only a very simple form of test was made. The pack of cards was shown to the subject about to be tested and the experimenter then explained to him that he would be asked to identify each card in turn, whilst it lay on the table in front of him, face downwards. The experimenter then seated himself opposite to the subject, and the pack was shuffled and placed face downwards on the table. The subject was then asked to state the symbol on the top card and after his call had been recorded on paper the named card was removed. Neither the experimenter nor the subject was allowed to look at the card in order to find out what symbol it actually bore. The next card was then named, the call recorded and the card removed; and this process was repeated until the whole pack had been gone through in like manner. Only then were the cards looked at and the scoring noted with the help of the previous record of the subject's guesses. Afterwards the pack was reshuffled and the whole process was repeated.

From chance alone the number of hits to be expected when using this kind of pack was five hits for every twenty-five cards named. If a subject scored above this average number of hits, the *deviation*, or number of hits *above* expectancy, was measured by the use of a mathematical yardstick known as the 'standard deviation'. This measure revealed what were the odds *against* chance alone being responsible for the score being higher than five in every twenty-five cards. If, for example, a subject had made four runs through the pack and had scored, not the average five per run to be expected, but an average of 7.5 hits per run, then the odds against this being the result merely of accident would be about 150 to 1 against.

The results of these tests carried out at Duke University were published in 1934. As already stated, chance alone would account for an average score of five hits per twenty-five guesses, but when all the results were pooled it was found that an average of seven per twenty-five guesses had been attained. This was a very remarkable result when it is remembered that the subjects had not been specially selected and that the unsuccessful performers as well as the successful ones were included in this list. Moreover, great care was always exercised to exclude the possibility that the subject had been assisted in any way by sensory impressions when he was naming the cards. The first precaution taken to exclude all help from sensory impressions was the placing of an opaque screen between the subject and the agent or experimenter, and at a later date the two were placed in different rooms. But sometimes all these elaborate precautions took their toll by rendering the subject less at his ease, and it soon became obvious to those who acted as experimenters that if too many restrictions were imposed on their subjects, the scores were likely to fall.

The first two series of tests carried out at Duke University were concerned with Extra-Sensory Perception in general and they gave no information on the subject of Telepathy as opposed to Clairvoyance. They did not give this because the experimenters were as ignorant of the identity of the card about to be guessed as were their subjects. This meant that no telepathic message was able to pass between them, and in order to make this possible and to render the test applicable to Telepathy, a change of technique had to be made. All that was required was that the agent should select *mentally* a symbol as soon as he had received from the subject a signal to indicate that he was ready to make his guess. The subject then made a note on a piece of paper of the symbol which had come into his mind after he had given the agent his readiness signal. Only *after* the subject had made this note and *after* the agent had received a signal that the subject was ready for the next *guess*, was the agent allowed to jot down on paper the symbol of which he had previously thought. If he had entered it on paper at any earlier moment, there was always the possibility that the subject would have obtained information by clairvoyance rather than by telepathy. At first the sender and receiver of the messages were seated in the same room, but later on they were placed successively, in different rooms, in different buildings and finally in different towns. The sender was trained to select his symbols in random order and, at a later date, a special method was devised which reduced the intervention in the agent's choice of personal preferences and of habitual modes of thought. This was of some importance for it might well happen that the agent thought more readily of crosses than of wavy lines, and, if the subject happened to have the same unconscious preferences, the two partialities would increase the likelihood of high scoring.

Some of the scoring obtained in the Telepathy tests was as high as that which had previously been recorded in the clairvoyance tests. Particularly striking scores were obtained by two women, Miss Ownberg and

Miss Turner, with Miss Ownberg acting as agent or transmitter and with Miss Turner as subject or recipient. When the two women were seated in the same room and every possible precaution had been taken to prevent sensory impressions from playing any part in Miss Turner's choice, she obtained an average of eight hits per run in a total of 275 calls. When the two were working at a distance of 250 miles from each other, Miss Turner obtained an average of ten hits per run in a total of eight runs through the pack, or 200 calls. Having reached this peak Miss Turner's scores steadily declined but, as has previously been pointed out, this is a very common event in parapsychological laboratory experiments.

Controlled experiments have shown that distance makes no difference to the results obtained from telepathy tests. This was particularly obvious in the long-distance experiments arranged between the students at Tarkir College, Missouri and those who were working at Duke University. The Zener cards were exposed at these two colleges at stated times, in the way that Carrington's drawings had been exposed, and the results were afterwards mailed to the senders of the telepathic messages. A number of long-distance tests of this kind, with the agents and the subjects separated from each other by anything from a few miles to several thousand miles, confirmed the fact, already noted, that distance had no influence at all on the results.

The Selection of Suitable Subjects

Attempts were also made at Duke University, and

elsewhere, to discover what are the personal characteristics which are likely to be associated with a high scoring ability. The conditions which are favourable to telepathy and are unfavourable to it have likewise been investigated but little progress has been made on these important subjects. It is known, of course, that all depressant drugs, of the sodium amytal variety, are likely to lead to a lowering of the score and that stimulants, such as caffeine, have a beneficial effect more especially when the subject has arrived for his tests rather tired or depressed. So also may a little alcohol help those who suffer from stage-fright before undergoing their tests. Emotional upsets almost always lead to deterioration of a subject's performance in the laboratory. Boredom has an equally bad effect and J. Langdon-Davies reports that he was compelled to replace his old pack of ESP cards with a fresh pack decorated with new drawings in order to revive a young Spanish nurse's interest in the tests which she had been undergoing for many weeks. Dr. E. S. Soal, who has a great deal of experience of card-guessing tests, makes the following comment on this tendency for the quality of performances to deteriorate when a subject becomes bored with card-guessing. 'Why so many good card-guessers should peter out and seemingly lose their ability in a short time is one of the major puzzles in psychical research. Time and again it has happened that someone who, over a period of two or three years, has been guessing above chance to the tune of astronomical odds, has suddenly within a few weeks, lost every vestige of paranormal faculty. Sooner or later, this has happened to every subject who has been investigated in England and America. It is all the more strange because good trance mediums, like Mrs. Piper and Mrs. Leonard, have retained their telepathic powers for twenty or thirty years. If parapsychology is to make any real progress, it will be essential for us to discover why significant, positive scoring suddenly disappears, or is replaced by negative scoring, and to find out the conditions under which a good subject can maintain extra-chance results over a considerable period.'[1]

Dr. Soal's Experiments with Mrs. Stewart and Mr. Basil Shackleton.

Dr. Soal was fortunate to have had the help of two exceptionally brilliant subjects in his work, namely, Mrs. G. Stewart and Mr. Basil Shackleton. He describes how the latter offered his assistance at a moment when he, Dr. Soal, was feeling very much dispirited by his failures to obtain any positive evidence either for clairvoyance or for telepathy. He had been working hard for over five years with many different subjects, he had recorded 128,350 guesses and yet he had nothing to show for all this hard labour. The only figures which could be called positive were those which he had obtained in certain experiments with Mrs. G. Stewart and even these figures were in no way remarkable. Then one gloomy November afternoon in 1936, Mr. Basil Shackleton, a photographer by profession, presented himself and informed Dr. Soal that he had demonstrated to his friends his very great capacity for

[1] S. G. Soal and F. Bateman, *Modern Experiment in Telepathy.*

telepathy. Dr. Soal was so impressed by Shackleton's confidence in himself that he agreed to test him. Alas, the score which he obtained with Shackleton was no higher than could be accounted for by chance alone and this served only to confirm the opinion to which Dr. Soal had previously come, that it was practically impossible – at any rate in England – to find any subject amongst students who could demonstrate ESP capacity by guessing Zener cards.

Then one of those very fortunate accidents occurred which happen so frequently in the history of scientific research, an accident which converted what had previously appeared to be a dismal sequence of failures into a brilliant sequence of successes. Dr. Soal was discussing with Whateley Carrington his long succession of failures when the latter interrupted him and brought to his notice his own experience, namely that a *displacement in time* often occurred in experimental work of this kind. He said that he had discovered the tendency of a subject to guess drawings which had been pinned up in his study the day before or the day afterwards, and not the drawing which was being exhibited on that actual day. In other words, he drew Dr. Soal's attention to the all important phenomenon of time displacement. He did more than this, for he insisted that Dr. Soal should immediately go through all his old experimental data again. He had to do this and he had to compare every guess, not only with the card the subject was supposed to be guessing, but also with the cards which had immediately preceded it and which immediately followed it. Having done all this he must regard as successful correct guesses of the cards preceding and following the card actually to be named. 'For', wrote Dr. Soal afterwards, 'according to Carrington, the faculty of extra-sensory cognition might not function in such a way that the subject always hit the target at which he was aiming. Just as a rifleman may show a personal bias which causes him persistently to strike the target at a point to the left or the right of the bull's eye, so it might happen that the guesser at Zener cards, all unwittingly, was guessing correctly, not the card the experimenter was looking at, but a card which was one or two places earlier or later in sequence.'

Very reluctantly Dr. Soal undertook the tedious task which Carrington had set him. He went through the records of Mrs. Stewart's guesses again and he soon discovered that Carrington had been right and that Mrs. Stewart had often guessed the identity of the card which had been turned up previously or which was about to be turned up. This factor of time displacement has now been widely recognized and it has become customary to record a hit made on the following card as a ($+1$) hit and a hit on the immediately preceding card as a (-1) hit. Long before Dr. Soal had completed his re-survey of Mrs. Stewart's seemingly negative results, he realized how profitable was Carrington's advice. His re-examination of the old notes revealed the existence of 221 post-cognitive (-1) hits as compared with the 192 (-1) hits to be expected from the action of accident alone. The correct pre-cognitive ($+1$) guesses were also well above chance expectations, namely 225 instead of 192. Dr. Soal was apprehensive lest the above-chance scoring would start diminishing in the way that so many of his positive findings had diminished as the experiments proceeded, but on this occasion his fears were not realized. On re-examining the records of Mrs. Stewart's later tests he found that the pre- and the post-cognitive hits actually increased a little, rising to 221 and 232 respectively.

It was not until December 1939, that Dr. Soal possessed sufficient leisure to go through the Shackleton records again, and he was delighted to find a time displacement there also, similar to that which he had previously found in the old Stewart records: 'On the target (0) card the deviation (+5) was not in the least significant but the pre-cognitive (+1) card there were 194 hits, and on the post-cognitive (—1) cards 195 hits, as compared, in each case, with a chance expectation of 153 and 156 respectively'. Dr. Soal tells us that after he had completed his survey of Mr. Shackleton's guesses he calculated that the odds against Shackleton's hits being the result of accident alone were as high as 2,500 to 1 against.

Encouraged by these striking results, and with the valuable assistance of Mrs. K. M. Goldney, Dr. Soal continued his experiments with Mr. Shackleton as his subject. Even stricter precautions were taken against the intervention of sensory aids in this new series. The agent and the subject were closely watched by two additional experimenters and this meant that, unless the whole party were conspiring together to perpetrate a fraud, any idea that the results were being obtained through sensory channels could be ruled out. Fresh information was also obtained about the conditions likely to exert either an adverse or a helpful influence on the subject's guesses. If we accept the idea that ESP exists – and only a prejudiced individual is able any longer to reject this idea – it is much more likely to be a product of the Subliminal Self than of the more conscious regions of the mind. This means that the subject who manifests ESP has very little control over the faculty and that its action is likely to be erratic. Dr. Soal tells us that he made changes in the laboratory procedure from time to time without having previously told the subject about it, and that these changes were often followed by negative results, where positive results had previously been recorded. So also were the characters and the behaviour of the agents important factors in the experiments. Soal made use of as many as a dozen different agents in the course of the Shackleton tests and Shackleton was successful with only three of them. The rate of the card-calling also had an effect on Shackleton's results. For example, if the speed of the card-calling were doubled he was likely to score not, as before, on the card immediately ahead of the target, (+1) card, but on the card two ahead of it (+2) card. As a rule, Shackleton was told beforehand whether it was his clairvoyance or his telepathic ability which was to be tested on that day, and it soon became apparent to everybody that his capacity for telepathy was far greater than was his capacity for clairvoyance. Indeed, the clairvoyance tests gave results which might have been accounted for by accident alone, whereas the odds against chance being responsible for his telepathic results were as high as ten million to one against. It was not lack of confidence which accounted for the poorness of Shackleton's clairvoyance tests, for he approached both varieties of test with equal assurance. Dr. Soal is inclined to attribute the difference to the marked time displacement factor which was so characteristic of Shackleton's work. As has already been shown, a great many experimenters have found that results deteriorated whenever their subjects were in a poor state of health, but this was never true of Shackleton. Dr. Soal reports that he frequently complained of ill-health, and of such troubles as 'bad nerves' and headaches, yet he still continued to obtain high scores. But he resembled other subjects in getting poor results whenever he became bored with card-guessing which, after all, is not a very interesting occupation. When this happened he sometimes obtained what could be called *negative* results, that is to say, results which were well *below* those attributable to chance alone. Now if an individual persistently chooses the wrong card and scores well below chance expectation, it is reasonable to suppose that part of his mind knows the identity of the card but, for some reason or other, decides *not* to name it. Negative, below-chance scoring of this kind occasionally occurred with Shackleton when he was obtaining high positive scores on the $(+1)$ and on the (-1) card, whilst working at ordinary speeds and on the $(+2)$ and (-2) cards whilst working at higher speeds. Dr. Soal is of the opinion that Shackleton's negative scoring on these occasions 'was due to a psychological reaction on his part which led him to change his call immediately after he had scored a pre-cognitive $(+1)$ hit.'

Rhine has also made an interesting comment on negative, below-chance scoring. He states that it can often be manifested in a previously high scoring subject if he is requested to avoid making any more hits. Rhine's highest scoring subject, Hubert Pearce, possessed this capacity, and Hubert Pearce must be considered a champion card-guesser. On one occasion he achieved a sequence of twenty-five correct guesses in a series of thirty-five calls, a level of performance he was never able to repeat. His capacity for card-guessing left him quite suddenly. He arrived one morning at the laboratory, after having received a depressing letter, and announced that he would not be likely to be of any use to them on that particular day. His prediction was only too true. After a few flashes of his old ability, his capacity for card-guessing departed for good, so that he was no longer a suitable subject for parapsychological tests.

Dr. Soal's Telepathy Experiments with the Jones Boys

The most recent experiments on telepathy reported in this country were those carried out by Dr. Soal with the help of two Welsh boys. He has described these Welsh tests in a book entitled, *The Mind Readers*. In 1936, Dr. Soal had made certain card-guessing tests on three brothers, Tom, Richard and Will Jones. They were living in a remote Welsh village and these earlier experiments had all been of the clairvoyance type. The tests had yielded scores very little, if anything, above what chance could account for. In spite of the poorness of the results, Dr. Soal remained of the opinion that better subjects for testing were to be found in the rural communities of England and Wales than in the student circles of University cities and, with this in his mind, he returned to Wales in 1955, taking with him a pack of Zener cards bearing the pictures of five different kinds of animals: a lion, a zebra, an elephant, a giraffe and a penguin. On arriving at the village he had visited before, he chose for his subjects two members of the next generation of Jones, two boys who bore the Christian names of Ierian and Glyn. They were first cousins and, at that time, they were fifteen years of age. The great majority of the experiments on the Jones boys were carried out in Wales and in a very small cottage. This meant that they were made under rather difficult conditions, for sometimes another member of the Jones family had to be present at the test. For a week the two boys came to London and on those occasions the tests were carried out in the library of the Society for Psychical Research. In order to encourage the boys to do their best, Dr. Soal started by offering a prize for all scoring above the 8/25 level. He thought it unlikely that they would earn very much money in this way, but at the end of his visit he was presented with two bills, amounting to over fifteen pounds, and he was glad to be able to reach a compromise with two five pound notes.

Many tests were made in Wales and in London during the next two years, some of them conducted by Dr. Soal himself and some by his colleague, Mr. Bowden. As has previously been pointed out, the score to be expected from chance alone, in a run through the whole pack of twenty-five cards, is 5/25 and in one of the tests, Glyn Jones managed to obtain fifty per cent of correct guesses. The usual precautions were taken against knowledge being passed from one boy to the other, either accidentally or intentionally through the special senses, and this presented some difficulty owing to the cramped quarters in which the experiments were being carried out. Because of this the experiments on the Jones boys have come in for very heavy criticism and, in the opinion of the author of this book, this criticism has not always been justified. What supports rather than weakens this view of the Jones boys experiments is the fact that on the one occasion in which the boys did actually resort to trickery, it was of so unskilful a nature that it was promptly detected.

A great number of carefully controlled experiments have now been carried out with cards, in many different countries, and in many different circumstances for the sole purpose of proving or disproving – so far as a negative can be disproved – the existence of clairvoyance and telepathy. Having examined much of this evidence, I find it difficult to doubt any longer the genuineness of these two psychic phenomena. So far as I can see, the experiments which have been specially devised for this purpose cannot be attacked, either on methodological grounds or because insufficient precautions have been taken to eliminate sensory cues influencing results. It is highly unlikely that all of these well-known experimenters have been deliberately engaged in perpetrating a fraud and that they have been so highly successful in their nefarious work that no fraud has as yet been detected by their many ardent critics. I have been personally assured by Dr. Soal himself that the statistical methods of dealing with the data obtained from card-guessing are as sound as those which have been used in other departments of science.

The situation is, however, much less clear when we turn from the subject of the tests and try to find an answer to the difficult question: How do clairvoyance and telepathy work? Here I think it better to return an honest answer and to reply quite simply: 'As yet we do not know.' All that can be done is to put forward certain suggestions about these phenomena, suggestions which will be made and discussed in later chapters.

5

Prophetic Dreams

The belief has always existed that changes in the level of consciousness, such as the familiar changes from wakefulness to sleep and from sleep back again to wakefulness, bring about alterations in our capacity to see and to understand things. For example, many people have claimed that there is a state midway between sleep and wakefulness in which their most inventive ideas have come to them. So also was it assumed in ancient China, Egypt, Judea and Greece that divinatory powers were often conferred on a person who slept in the neighbourhood of one of the great temples and much of the therapeutic treatment in the temples of Aesculapius was based on this belief. Professor Guthrie writes: 'To the Asklepieia came many sick persons for the healing ritual known as "mentation" or "temple sleep". On arrival the patient was expected to make a sacrificial offering and to purify himself by bathing. Then he lay down to sleep on the *abaton*, a long colonnade open to the air at each side. During the night Aesculapius appeared in a dream, and gave advice or in certain cases performed an operation, and in the morning the patient then departed cured.' He does not add, what is highly probable, that the temple priests also appeared on the *abaton* at night and whispered certain suggestions in the ears of the sleepy patients. Professor Guthrie also tells us that traces of the old temple rituals and practices are still to be found in the

Greek islands and on the Mediterranean coast: 'In the churches of Palermo, Naples, Sardinia and Styria the custom survives to this day. On the sacred island of Tenos, close to Delos, a great religious festival is held twice a year, and many sick persons sleep in the church in expectation of a cure.'[1]

So also has it long been believed that the future is often foreshadowed in a dream. Many examples of prophetic dreams could be given. Pharaoh's dream in which he stood before a river (representing *time*), out of which came seven well-favoured kine and afterwards seven lean-fleshed kine, is a well-known example of a prophetic dream. Dreams of this kind arise in the Subliminal Self and because this region of the mind makes great use of symbols, they often have to be interpreted. Pharaoh had no doubt that his dreams would have to be interpreted and he promptly sent for his magicians. But for some strange reason Pharaoh's wise men failed to discover the meaning of his dream, a meaning which was immediately apparent to the bright Hebrew lad, Joseph. So also is Calpurnia's dream on the night before Caesar's assassination an excellent example of a prophetic dream. In her dream Calpurnia saw the statue of her husband spouting blood, a dream whose meaning was so obvious that no interpretation was required.

A modern counterpart of these old prophetic dreams is the dream which Abraham Lincoln had a week or two before his own assassination. He gives the following account of it:

[1] Douglas Guthrie, *A History of Medicine.*

'There seemed to be a deathlike stillness about me . . . then I heard subdued sobs, as if a number of people were weeping. I thought I left my bed and wandered downstairs. There, the silence was broken by the same pitiful sobbing but the mourners were invisible. I went from room to room; no living person was inside, but the same mournful sounds of distress met me as I passed along. I was puzzled and alarmed. What could be the meaning of all this . . . ? I arrived at the East room which I entered . . . There I met a sickening surprise. Before me was a catafalque on which rested a corpse in funeral vestments. Around it were stationed soldiers who were acting as guards; and there was a throng of people, some gazing mournfully upon the corpse, whose face was covered, others weeping pitifully. "Who is dead in the White House?" the dreamer asks. "The President . . . He was killed by an assassin."' According to Ward Hill Laman's report of what happened Lincoln brought to an end his account of his dream with these revealing words: 'I slept no more that night and was strangely annoyed by the dream ever since.'[1]

Yet another precognitive dream will be given, not because it is more dramatic than Abraham Lincoln's dream, but because it possesses certain features which throw light on the manner in which prophetic dreams are produced. The subject of this dream had this in common with Abraham Lincoln, that he also was an historical figure and that he was the victim of assassination. He was Spencer Perceval, Prime Minister and Chancellor of the Exchequer, who was shot in the

[1] Quoted by Jan Ehrenfeld in *Telepathy and Medical Psychology*.

lobby of the House of Commons on 11 May 1812. The dream is described by a medical man, a Dr. John Abercrombie, in a book which was published in 1838 under the somewhat misleading title, *Inquiries Concerning the Intellectual Powers*. Dr. Abercrombie writes:

'Through the kindness of an eminent medical friend in England, I have received the authentic particulars of this remarkable case, from the gentleman to whom the dream occurred. He resides in Cornwall and, eight days before the murder was committed, he dreamt that he was in the lobby of the House of Commons, and saw a small man enter, dressed in a blue coat and white waistcoat. Immediately after, he saw a man dressed in a brown coat with yellow basket metal buttons, draw a pistol from under his coat, and discharge it at the former, who instantly fell – the blood issuing from a wound a little below the left breast. He saw the murderer seized by some gentlemen who were present, and observed his countenance; and on asking who the gentleman was who had been shot, he was told it was the Chancellor. (Mr. Perceval was, at that time, Chancellor of the Exchequer.) He then awoke and mentioned the dream to his wife, who made light of it – but in the course of the night the dream occurred three times without the least variation in any of the circumstances. He was now so much impressed by it, that he felt much inclination to give notice to Mr. Perceval, but was dissuaded by some friends whom he consulted, who assured him he would only get himself treated as a fanatic. On the evening of the eighth day after, he received the account of the murder. Being in London a short time after, he found in the print-shops a representation of the scene, and recognized in it the countenance and dress of the parties, the blood on Mr. Perceval's waistcoat, and the peculiar yellow basket buttons on Bellingham's (the murderer's) coat, precisely as he had seen them in his dream.'[1]

W. H. Sabine, from whose book I have taken the account of this prophetic dream, makes the following comments on it. He first points out that despite the vividness and the repetition of the dream, no effective steps were taken to warn the Prime Minister of his danger. He then goes on to say that we are left in doubt whether the dreamer's foreknowledge was of the actual assassination of Mr. Perceval or of his subsequent discovery and examination of a coloured print which portrayed that assassination. Mr. Sabine himself thinks the latter to be the more likely explanation of it and he states that many other examples could be given of the precognition of reports of events published afterwards in newspapers, rather than of the actual events themselves. The fact that the narrator of the story of the dream about Spencer Perceval's assassination takes pains to point out to the reader that the dream corresponded very closely with the print subsequently examined suggests that he also believed that the *dream* foreshadowed the seeing of the print rather than the actual assassination.

In 1917 a book was written by J. W. Dunne which quickly established itself as a best-seller and which ran through several editions. It was entitled, *An Experiment in Time* and it contained not only accounts of many

[1] W. H. Sabine, *Second Sight in Daily Life.*

precognitive dreams, but also a theory of time which
in Dunne's opinion, explained what had happened.
Only two of the many precognitive dreams recounted
by Dunne will be selected for discussion. The first was
a dream which he had in 1904 whilst on a holiday in
Austria. Dunne writes of it as follows:

'I dreamed one night that I was walking down a sort
of pathway between two fields separated from the latter
by high iron railings, eight or nine feet high, on each
side of the path. My attention was suddenly attracted
to a horse in the field on the *left*. It had apparently gone
mad, and was tearing about, kicking and plunging in
a most frenzied fashion. I cast a hasty glance backwards
and forwards along the railings to see if there were any
openings by which the animal could get out. Satisfied
that there were none, I continued on my way. A few
moments later I heard hoofs thundering behind me.
Glancing back I saw, to my dismay, that the brute *had*
somehow got out after all, and was coming full tilt after
me down the pathway. It was a full-fledged nightmare
– and I ran like a hare. Ahead of me the path ended at
the foot of a flight of wooden steps rising upwards. I was
striving frantically to reach these when I awoke.'

Dunne tells us that the next day he went fly-fishing
on a little river and that whilst industriously flogging
the water with his line his brother called out 'Look at
that horse!' He continues his story thus. 'Glancing
across the river, I saw the scene of my dream. *But
though right in essentials, it was absolutely unlike in minor
details*. The two fields with the fenced-off pathway
running between them were there. The horse was there,
behaving just as it had done in the dream. The wooden

steps at the end of the pathway were there (they led up to a bridge crossing the river). But the fences were wooden and small – not more than four or five feet high – and the fields were ordinary small fields, whereas those in the dream had been park-like expanses. Moreover, the horse was a small beast, and not the rampaging great monster of the dream – though its behaviour was equally alarming. Finally, it was in the wrong field, the field which would have been on my *right*, had I been walking, as in the dream, down the path towards the bridge. I began to tell my brother about the dream, but broke off because the beast was behaving so very oddly that I wanted to make sure that it could not escape. As in the dream, I ran my eye critically along the railings. As in the dream, I could see no gap, or even gate, in them anywhere. Satisfied, I said, "At any rate *this* horse cannot get out," and recommenced fishing. But my brother interrupted me by calling "Look out!" Glancing up again, I saw that there was no dodging fate. The beast *had*, inexplicably, just as in the dream, got out (probably it had jumped the fence), and, just as in the dream, it was thundering down the path towards the wooden steps. It swerved past these and plunged into the river, coming straight towards us. We both picked up stones, ran thirty yards or so back from the bank, and faced about. The end was tame, for, on emerging from the water on our side, the animal merely looked at us, snorted and galloped off down the road.'[1]

Many interesting points arise in discussing this dream. In the first place it shows that precognitive dreams are

[1] J. W. Dunne, *An Experiment with Time.*

not necessarily concerned with important events or with impending disasters. More often than not they are dreams of a very commonplace nature, dreams woven around some trivial waking experience which would never have received any attention had they occurred *after* the waking experience on which they were founded had taken place. But dreams of this precognitive nature happen *before* the experience has occurred and it is only when the experience has actually taken place that the precognitive dream assumes importance and that it can sometimes be recalled. A second example of a precognitive dream taken from Dunne's book will make this clearer. He recounts how, whilst convalescing from an operation in Guy's Hospital, he was reading a book which gave a description of one of those old fashioned combination locks which are opened by manipulating a number of rings on which are embossed the letters of the alphabet. As he read the description of this kind of lock, something seemed to stir in his mind, but he could not think at first what it was that had stirred. He paused, resumed reading his book and then threw it aside, for he had suddenly recalled that on the *previous* night he had dreamed of a lock of that nature. Could it be a pure coincidence? This was unlikely, for he had not come across, heard of or read about that particular kind of lock for many years.

Dunne's dream about the lettered lock had certain features in common with those of his dream about the horse, and now that he was on the lookout for this kind of phenomenon he was to have many similar precognitive dreams in the course of the following years. As a result of his keeping a very careful note of all of his dreams and of his being on the lookout for similar events occurring during the subsequent waking hours, Dunne was coming to the conclusion that a *time* displacement frequently took place in dreams so that they were often related to *future* and not to *past* events in his life. Because the subsequent events were often of a very trivial nature, the connexion between them and the previous dream would have been missed had he not made a practice of making a note of all his dreams immediately on awakening from sleep. He put down on paper not only his dreams but also his first thoughts after opening his eyes, for he found that thoughts often led him back to what he had previously been dreaming about. Because he was trying to establish a connexion between incidents in his dream and incidents occurring in the awakened state during the following few days, the more unusual the events recorded in his dreams, the more likely it was that he would notice similar unexpected events in his subsequent waking hours. But he had to be very careful, for he found that the mind responsible for his dreams was an adept at tacking false interpretations on to everything it perceived. This being so he made a practice of recording not only as many of the details of the dream as possible but also the interpretation which he had given to the dream immediately on awakening from it.

The quickness with which a dream was forgotten was not the only or the greatest difficulty with which Dunne had to contend. He found that his waking mind often played tricks on him and refused to see any connexion between the dream and the subsequent causative event. It was blind to this connexion for the simple reason that cause and effect were being viewed the wrong way round, the dream-incident having preceded the day-incident which caused it. In other words, the *effect* preceded in time its *cause* and this was highly confusing to a mind conditioned to think always in terms of the cause preceding its effect. The main object of Dunne's earlier experiments was to discover whether the faculty of precognition was a normal characteristic of the human mind, or whether it should be regarded – as many people regarded it – as being a paranormal or unusual activity of man's mind. The outcome of the many experiments carried out with the help of his friends, was to the effect that precognition was an entirely normal psychic phenomenon and that it occurred far more often than people imagined it did.

The next question which Dunne asked himself was: 'But why should precognition work only in dreams? Why should it not occur also when we are awake?' Why not indeed? Might not this explain many other things such as the phenomenon called by the French the *déjà vu* phenomenon, that is to say the feeling we sometimes have 'that all this has happened before'. Dunne now set out to experiment on this new aspect of precognition, that it might occur in a state of wakefulness. He selected for reading a new book from a bookshelf, and sat down and thought determinedly, for a time, about the significance of the book's title. He did this in order to start his reading with a leading idea in his head, an idea which would be likely to establish associational links with whatever was to turn up later when he was actually reading the book. He then waited for odds and ends in the way of words and mental images to come into his mind through the automatic process of association. Naturally it was of the utmost importance that he should be certain that he had never read the book previously and subsequently forgotten the fact that he had read it. The results of these association experiments with books were highly erratic and likely to be negative, but occasionally they were sufficiently near the mark to allow of their being accepted as positive. Dunne makes the following comment on his book experiments: 'These experiments showed me that, provided one were able to "steady" one's attention to the task, one could observe the "effect" just as readily when awake as when sleeping. But that "steadying" of attention is no easy matter. It is true that it makes no call upon a special faculty but it does demand a great deal of practice in controlling the imagination. Hence to anyone who is desirous merely of satisfying himself as to the existence of the "effect" I should recommend the dream-recording experiment in preference to the waking attempt.'

When assessing the results of his dream experiments, Dunne divides his positive results into two categories, those in which the dream corresponded with an event which lay in the *future* and those in which the dream corresponded with an event lying in the *past*, and he called these two categories F-resemblances and P-resemblances respectively. He expected that the P-resemblances would greatly outnumber the F-resemblances, but in the eighty-eight experiments made the reverse of this happened. The six subjects taking part in this series of experiments dreamed more of events to happen in the future than of events which had happened in the past. This tendency of Dunne's subjects to dream more of the future than of the past is probably explained by their ages, for the average age of Dunne's six collaborators worked out at only twenty-one, and it is well known that the young are prone to look forward, whilst the elderly tend to look back at their past.

On the basis of his various experiments, Dunne has propounded a theory of time which has not found favour with many philosophers. It is Dunne's experiments and not his theory of time which is of importance to us, and it is of interest to note that the former support the view which has already been expressed several times in this book, that *precognition* is not a highly unusual phenomenon but a comparatively common one.

Max Freedom Long, the expounder of the South Sea Island or 'Huna' philosophy has confirmed Dunne's view that dreams are frequently precognitive. He describes in his book, *The Secret Science Behind Miracles*, a dream of which he made brief but careful notes immediately on awakening from it. The hastily made notes ran as follows:

'Strange big fattish man. Came to me and asked if I would help him on an invention – something of an optical nature . . . Was at my desk. Had before me a piece of a smallish machine, about two feet six inches by four inches in size. Black electrical cord and white one running from the rear end of the thing. It looked like a black enamelled lid. In a side of this lid or cap was a square hole about four inches by four inches. On the top of the lid was an hourglass-shaped set-screw of blued steel. (I made a rough drawing here, of the lid.) . . . I was in a latticed low kitchen. Fat man there.

Stranger was there, tall, slim, light, and about forty. Small Hawaiian woman there. I took sensitive paper from a box and placed it in a small opening in the machine. The thin man touched a switch and a light flashed. I took out the paper and developed it in one of three strange little white photo trays. The developed image was a scale, and a pointer which indicated a large number. I looked at the men. We laughed. I said, "Well, it works."

'That was on Sunday night. On the following Thursday afternoon the dreams began to come true. The fat man I had seen in my dreams came into my camera store. He wanted help in splitting a ray of light to get an image of a weight-scale on a ground glass screen and a strip of recording photo paper at the same time. The top of the mechanism of the scale was described to me. It checked with the lid I had seen in my dream. I agreed to help him.

'The next part of my dream was wrong. The lid was never brought to me and I never had it before me on my desk. I did not see it until after the mechanism I worked out, and which was built in a local machine shop, was completed. I saw it later, however, in the latticed kitchen of my dream. The tall, light man of my dream was the mechanic on the job, and it was his kitchen. The small Hawaiian woman was also there. She was his wife. The machine was used for weighing sugar syrup in sugar refineries.'[1]

Dreams possess interesting features in addition to the fact that they are often precognitive. They may be of

[1] Max Freedom Long, *The Secret Science Behind Miracles*.

a highly artistic nature, a fact to which Ouspensky
long ago drew attention. He wrote that by studying
his dreams he had discovered within himself 'an artist,
sometimes very naïve, sometimes very subtle, who
worked at these dreams and created them out of
material which he possessed but could never use in
full measure when awake'. He added that the artist
hidden within him was 'extraordinarily versatile in
his knowledge, capacities and talents'. The artist to
which Ouspensky is here referring is of course his own
Subliminal Self in which reside those highly creative
little people and Brownies described by Robert Louis
Stevenson. The Subliminal Self is likewise the abode of
that tireless and admirable basement worker known to
the students of the *Huna* culture by the unromantic
name of 'George'. Yet another interesting characteristic
of dreams is the speed with which they unroll themselves.
Ouspensky quotes an excellent example of this, an
example which he obtained from L. F. A. Maury's
book, *Sleep and Dreams*.[1] Maury describes how he was
lying in his bed, slightly indisposed and with his
mother in his room for the purpose of looking after
him. He states that in these circumstances and in the
presence of his mother, he had the following dream:
'I am dreaming of the Terror . . . I appear before the
Revolutionary Tribunal; I see Robespierre, Marat,
Fouquier-Turville, all the most villainous figures of
this terrible epoch; I argue with them; at last, after
many events which I remember only vaguely, I am
judged, condemned to death, taken in a cart amidst

[1] L. F. A. Maury, *Le Sommeil et les Rêves*.

an enormous crowd to the square of the Revolution;
I ascend the scaffold, the executioner binds me to the
fatal board, he moves it, the knife falls; I feel my head
being severed from my body; I awake seized by the
most violent terror, and I feel on my neck the rod of
the bed, which had suddenly become detached and
had fallen on my neck. This happened in one instant,
as my mother confirmed to me, and yet it was this
external sensation that was taken by me for the starting
point of the dream, with a whole series of successive
incidents'.[1]

Ouspensky makes two comments on Maury's dream.
He agrees with him that the whole dream unrolled
itself in the space of only a few seconds but he stresses
the still more interesting fact that the events in the
dream 'followed not in the order in which the dreamer
describes them but from the *end* towards the beginning'.
Consequently the actual sequence of events must have
been something like this: the rod falls; it evokes in
Maury an intense reaction of fear – 'What on earth
has happened to me?' Answer: 'I am being guillotined.'
The artist and dramatist in Maury's Subliminal Self
then produces the sequence of scenes required to render
the fact that he is being guillotined comprehensible;
the Paris crowds, the Tribunal, endless talk and
argument, his condemnation to death, the journey in
a cart to the Place de la Concorde, his head being
placed in position by the executioner. At this moment
Maury is awakened and he opens his eyes. He recalls
the memories of his dream but he places the scenes in

[1] Quoted by P. D. Ouspensky in *A New Model of the Universe*.

the only order in which they make sense to his awakened reason and not in the order in which they were actually dreamed. This entails that he should begin with the Paris crowds, his arrest and his appearance before the Tribunal.

It is only fair to the reader to add that all modern scientists are not agreed that dreams invariably unfold themselves with great speed. Some are of the opinion that dreams are occasionally much more leisurely in developing themselves than has been supposed.

6

Mind and Body

Much has been learnt about telepathy, clairvoyance and precognition during the last fifty years but when we attempt to fit these psychic activities into some general plan of the human mind we run up against insuperable difficulties. There are many gaps in that great jig-saw puzzle we call knowledge and one of the largest and most inconvenient of them is the gap between our knowledge of the body and our knowledge of the mind. No general understanding has ever been reached on this all-important subject of the body-mind relationship and all of us are entitled to reach our own conclusions about it. As will be seen later, I personally subscribe to the non-dualistic *advaita* philosophy of the Hindu, but I do not propose to inflict a description of it on the reader. All that it is necessary to point out is that none of us knows much about the subject which concerns us most deeply – our own nature. Our ignorance reveals itself in the most startling fashion whenever we attempt, as we are attempting now, to arrive at some general plan of the human mind. We discover that there is no such thing as an agreed plan of the mind, for each of us is interpreting the word 'mind' in a different way. The scientist interprets it in terms of matter and mechanism, the idealist in terms of thought and feeling and the psychologist in terms of the school of psychology to which he happens to belong. Even when we put aside the difficult philosophical question of the relationship of the body to the mind and study the mind in a state of isolation, very little agreement is to be found. One variety of psychologist abstracts certain 'psychisms' from the totality of the human *psyche* and combines them into an entity which he may call the 'ego' or the 'personality'. A second psychologist makes another set of abstractions and makes use of them in a similar fashion with the final result that we have not one but multiple systems of psychology. What adds to the confusion is that we make use of terms coined by these different schools, but we use them in different senses. For me, the 'ego' is that egoistic, separatist and self-centred element in myself which is the cause of a great many of my difficulties, but I have heard the same word 'ego' used to denote man's spiritual essence. The word 'personality' is subject to the same sort of confusion. For me, the word 'personality' stands for that complex of emotional, intellectual and movement habits which determines the great majority of my actions. The personality is the *persona* or mask behind which the ancient Greek and Roman actors played their allotted parts. But, in my case, my personality is far more likely to play *me* than *I* am to play it. It is obvious that other writers are using these two words 'ego' and 'personality' in an entirely different sense to that in which I am using it.

There being no general agreement on the body-mind problem, it will be necessary to give a brief summary of the various attitudes that may be adopted to it, starting with the attitude of that leader of modern thought – the scientist.

The Scientific View of Mind

The scientist attempts to explain everything, including life, mind and thought in terms of matter and mechanism, but the human mind is not lending itself readily to such a form of explanation, and now that the parapsychologists are claiming that telepathy, precognition and clairvoyance have also to be included in the general scheme, their difficulties have been increased a hundredfold. The scientists realize that it is quite impossible to explain these paranormal phenomena in terms of matter and mechanism, and, this being so, they have no alternative to that of denying their existence. They must not be blamed for doing this and for remaining faithful to the machine-model which has served them so well. It is, of course, true that quite apart from the difficulty caused by such anomalies as extra-sensory perception, certain objections were being brought against the machine-model of the universe by the physicists themselves but these were not of a very serious nature, and in all probability they would eventually be overcome. In the meantime, these difficulties in physics could be rendered less obtrusive by frankly admitting their existence and by giving them such names as Heisenberg's principles of uncertainty.

Long before the nature of the human mind began to puzzle the scientists it was a source of constant worry to the philosophers. How could two such entirely different entities as a material body, with mass and extension in space, and an immaterial mind with neither of these qualities, *meet* and *interact* on one another? The two had so little in common that it was difficult to see how they could make contact, let alone influence each other. This awkward question has been posed by philosophers for over two thousand years and no one has ever returned a really satisfactory answer to it. Yet there can be no doubt at all that body and mind do actually meet, react on each other and influence one another profoundly.

Where is their meeting ground? If we were to open a man's skull and to peer into it – a perfectly feasible proceeding at the present day – we should see the brain lying there underneath its glistening covering membrane. If we were then to remove a small piece of its friable substances for microscopic examination, we should find that the brain was made up of millions and millions of branching nerve-cells, all connected up with each other by means of their delicate branches. When the brain becomes active, chemico-physical changes occur in these cells and when the brain is at rest, as it is when we are sleeping, the cells recover and return to their former quiescent state. But is this all that a man really is, an elaborate piece of machinery which responds to a wonder-working computor housed within a man's head? Are our feelings, our thoughts, our hopes, our fears and our values only different manifestations of the chemical changes taking place in our brain cells? Can our searching for truth, our philosophizing, our theorizing, our writing and reading of books, all be resolved into changes occurring in the granules of pyramid-shaped nerve cells, changes which are no more relevant to what is true and what is false, than are the similar changes taking place during digestion in the cells lining our stomachs? Is this all that we really are?

I am unable to accept so monstrous a suggestion merely because I am unable to explain how two such alien entities as an immaterial mind and a material body meet and affect each other. I shall fall back instead on the idea that the physical changes in my brain cells and the mental phenomena association with those changes belong to two different worlds and that in spite of the difficulty I experience in explaining it, my mind and my body do actually meet and interact on one another.

Many philosophical solutions of this mind-body problem have been offered, some of them so naïve as to be, in the opinion of the writer of this book, quite absurd. There is the solution which was suggested by that great philosopher and mathematician, René Descartes. His method of dealing with the ancient problem was to start by declaring that the obstacles to bringing together two such incongruous objects as a material body and an immaterial mind were so great as to be insurmountable. This being so we must abandon the idea that the mind and the body did in fact meet and react on each other and replace it with the idea that they merely kept time with each other, like two perfectly synchronized clocks. Naturally Descartes's answer evokes in us another question. We immediately inquire of him how the two clocks of the mind and the body have managed to keep such perfect time with each other that we have been deceived into believing that there existed a cause-and-effect relationship between them. To this new question Descartes

would have replied that our minds and our bodies were
created by God and that they were wound up and set
going at precisely the same moment. As the result of
the Almighty's perfect craftsmanship and of His
equally perfect timing, each tick of the body has
synchronized with each tick of the mind ever since.
And we should be justified in rejecting Descartes's
explanation, for although philosophers may occasionally be excused for enlisting the aid of the Almighty
in getting out of their difficulties, they should resort to
this method as seldom as possible. In the opinion of the
author of this book, it would be much better for us to
reject Descartes's solution of the mind-body problem
and to reply quite simply, when questioned about this
relationship – 'Frankly, we don't know'.

When the gap between two entities which are known
to interact on each other is so wide that nothing can be
found to bridge it, we should always consider the
possibility that we have exaggerated the width of the
gap and should reduce it. In the present instance this
could be done either by making the mind a little more
like the body, or the body a little more like the mind.
This has been done by certain philosophers and notably
by Lord Russell, who regards the mind and the body as
having much more in common than we have imagined.
For him, mind and matter are different aspects of a
single antecedent entity, which possesses the qualities of
both mind and body. Although less explicit than Lord
Russell, Eddington would seem to have moved in the
same philosophical direction. He wrote 'that mind controlled, not only the atom, but atomic systems of all
degrees of complexity', and by this he surely meant that

matter was not the inert and mindless substance which some physicists believed it to be.

Personally I am of the opinion that we in the West have made far too broad a gap between mind and matter and that by depriving Nature of all mind we have reduced the universe to an insane jazz dance of particles. What is now demanded of us is that we should carry out an act of restitution, namely the act of restoring to Nature the qualities of which we have deprived her, the qualities of life and mind. In advocating this, I am following in the wake of that great and big-hearted philosopher, A. N. Whitehead, who wrote: 'Scientific reasoning is completely dominated by the presupposition that mental functionings are not properly a part of Nature . . . As a method, this procedure is entirely justified, provided that we recognize the limitations involved . . . Science can find no individual enjoyment in Nature; science can find no creativity in Nature; it finds merely rules of succession. These negations are true of natural science. They are inherent in its methodology. The reason for this blindness of physical science lies in the fact that such science only deals with half of the evidence provided by human experience . . . The disastrous separation of body and mind which has been fixed on European thought by Descartes is responsible for this blindness of science.'[1]

The bringing together of mind and matter may be confusing to us at first, but it is an idea which has always been favoured in the East. It found expression at least three thousand years ago in Hindu philosophy

[1] A. N. Whitehead, *Nature and Life*.

where it was taught that there exist subtle and highly
intelligent forms of matter, far too tenuous to be
perceptible to our special senses, even when these are
aided by scientific instruments such as the microscope
and the spectroscope. The finer bodies of man, known
to present-day Theosophists as the Astral, the Mental
and the Causal bodies are of this more subtle nature.
Formerly the Christian Church subscribed to this
doctrine, the finer bodies being called the Natural,
Spiritual and Divine bodies respectively. They were
said to pervade man's coarser carnal body in much the
same way that water pervades a sponge, and that the
still finer material of Oxygen may be dissolved in the
water filling the sponge. But there is an important
difference between theosophical teaching on this subject
and that of the original Eastern doctrine from which
this teaching came. Whereas the Theosophists pro-
claim that everyone possesses these finer bodies, the
older teaching was to the effect that they were developed
only in more highly evolved men.

Sri Aurobindo, who was educated in England and
in consequence of this often acted as a bridge between
Eastern and Western learning, summarizes, as follows,
the Indian teaching on the subject of the finer gradations of matter: 'All who have sounded these abysses
are agreed to bear witness to this fact that there are
series of subtler and subtler formulations of substance
which escape from, and go beyond, the formula of the
physical universe. Without going too deeply into
matters which are too difficult or occult for our present
inquiry, we may say . . . that these gradations of
substance, in one important aspect of their formulation

in series, can be seen to correspond to the ascending series of Matter, Life, Supermind and that other higher triplicity of *Sachchidananda*. In other words, we find that substance, in its ascension, bases itself upon each of these principles and makes itself successively a characteristic vehicle for the dominating cosmic self-expression of each in their ascending series.'[1]

The difficulties produced by Descartes disappear like morning mists, when we substitute a monist for a dualistic philosophy and, speaking personally, I have adopted a materialism of the Eastern variety described by Sri Aurobindo. It is a materialism entirely different from the materialism of the West. Whereas the latter degrades mind to the level of brute matter, the former raises matter to the level of mind. It proclaims that we live, not as the scientists suggest, in a clockwork and mindless universe but in a universe which is alive, and in which thought and consciousness are paramount forces.

Having discussed the various backgrounds against which the phenomena of telepathy, clairvoyance and precognition have to be viewed, we can now return to a study of the Unconscious Mind and the first question needing consideration is whether the human mind is capable of exerting any influence on matter lying outside the boundaries of the physical body. This claim has been made by some of the parapsychologists and it is said to have gained support from the carrying out of certain experiments.

Can the Mind affect Matter outside the limits of the Body?
We know that our minds exert their influence on our

[1] Sri Aurobindo, *The Life Divine*, vol. 1, p. 308.

bodies, for every moment we are demonstrating this fact. But can mind produce a direct effect on matter which lies outside the limits of our bodies? In the past, it was said that physical disturbances were sometimes associated with great emotional crises, as happened when the veil of the Temple was rent in twain. So also does Dr. Jung, during an emotional crisis, claim that there was an instance of a household article breaking in two during an emotional crisis in his earlier life. Some gamblers are convinced that their minds have been responsible on certain occasions for exerting an influence on the fall of dice. They believe that when the attention of a dice-thrower attains a certain degree of concentration and when he *wills* that the dice should fall in the way in which he wants them to fall, the dice sometimes obey his command. This, at any rate, was the belief which made Dr. Rhine decide to submit 'willed' dice-throwing to a scientific test and special experiments were devised for this purpose at Duke University. The question which had to be answered was whether or not the scores obtained after 'willing' dice to fall in a predetermined way were any higher than could be accounted for by chance alone. A number of different variations were made in the technique employed during the course of the many experiments which were carried out at Duke University. At the start, the dice were thrown by hand but later they were either ejected from a cup or else propelled on to the table by means of a suitable mechanical device. The number of dice ejected at every throw was also varied. The experiments started with the throwing of a single dice; then a pair was substituted for the single dice and afterwards six, twelve, twenty-four and forty-eight were ejected simultaneously on to the table. Rhine writes of these experiments as follows: 'If one dice were thrown, the target had to be one of six faces; if a pair, it might be a designated face or it might be a combination such as seven's, on a high dice (a total of eight to twelve), or on a low dice (a total of two to six).' Rhine reports that the majority of the earlier experiments yielded results which were sufficiently above chance expectation to encourage the experimenters to continue their investigation. 'More and more the realization grew that some other factor than chance was operating and it was a factor that could not be attributed to errors in recording, or to faulty dice, or to skill in throwing.'[1]

The Duke University dice-throwing tests were begun in 1934, broken off for a time, and then resumed in the year 1942. An examination of the total results obtained from these experiments showed that there were certain similarities between the results of these new PK tests, as they were called, and those previously obtained in the ESP tests. For example, it was found that in both cases the scoring tended to decline during the course of a run, the successes being more numerous at the beginning of it than at the end of it. So also were the results of varying the conditions of the tests carefully observed. For example, experiments were made in order to find out whether the number, the size and the weight of the dice affected the results. All that could be said with any certainty on this subject was that scoring was likely to be highest when the conditions were those which the subject favoured and found to be of the

[1] J. B. Rhine, *New World of the Mind*.

greatest interest to himself. In other words, the results seemed to have depended on the psychological rather than the physical conditions under which the experiments were carried out. Another similarity between the new PK tests and the older ESP tests was the effect which the taking of drugs was likely to have on them. In both cases large doses of sodium amytal or of alcohol lowered the scoring, whilst caffeine had the opposite effect, more especially when the subject was tired. So also were the results of hypnosis and of suggestion under hypnosis similar to those which had previously been noted in the ESP tests.

Another interesting similarity was that the phenomenon of time displacement occasionally appeared in the PK tests as it had previously appeared in the telepathy and extra-sensory tests. This statement requires however, qualification, for it is obvious that in dice-throwing displacement could not manifest itself in precisely the same manner as it had manifested itself in card-guessing, owing to the great difference in the techniques employed in the two forms of test. Displacement in dice-throwing manifested itself in the obtaining of combinations which were mentally, but not physically, adjacent to the score at which the subject was aiming. Rhine makes the following interesting comment on the relationship existing between extra-sensory perception and psycho-kinesis (PK), and from it we can see that he regards psycho-kinesis as being dependent to a great extent on clairvoyance: 'If we suppose that the mind of the subject in some way influences the roll of the dice by operating upon it in some point of space and time then ESP is a necessary part of the PK process. So decisive would this argument seem to be that if PK had been discovered without any previous knowledge of ESP, then the latter would have had to have been assumed in order to make the former intelligible . . . PK implies ESP and ESP implies PK.'

The Close Linkage between the different varieties of Paranormal Phenomena

Looking back now on the various paranormal phenomena of the mind which have been described and discussed in the earlier chapters of this book, we see that there is a very close similarity between them. First, we found that Telepathy and Clairvoyance had to be considered together because it was impossible to be sure which of the two was responsible for what was happening. Next, it was found that Precognition was often associated with Telepathy and that whilst Precognition took liberties with *time*, so also did Telepathy take liberties with *space*. Now, in the present chapter, we have discovered that the relationship between Extra-Sensory Perception and Psycho-kinesis is so intimate that the two phenomena cannot be separated from each other. It was on account of this tendency on the part of paranormal phenomena to flow together that Dr. Thouless and Dr. Weisner had suggested several years previously that they should all be regarded as being different manifestations of a single faculty of man: a faculty which might be designated by the Greek letter 'Psi'.

The Nature of the Different Manifestations of the Psi Factor

The final question to be discussed in this chapter is

whether the various ESP faculties in man should be regarded as being supernormal and in process of development or whether they are common to everybody. The answer to this question is that these faculties are not only natural to man but that they probably exist in varying degrees, in every living organism. Many naturalists have resorted to the ideas of telepathy and clairvoyance when attempting to explain the behaviour of gregarious birds, animals and insects. It is difficult to watch a flock of migrating birds manœuvring in the sky as a single unit, wheeling together, veering now in this direction, now in that, and maintaining the same flock pattern all the time, without feeling that they are linked together by something which is much more immediate and certain in its action than are the special senses. So also did I feel that something more than the special senses was in action when, as a young man, I lay for hours behind a bush watching the behaviour of zebra and antelope grazing in the Great Rift Valley of East Africa. I was convinced that these animals possessed a means of detecting my presence and of communicating their fears other than by sight, hearing and smell. Yet a note of caution has to be sounded here. The possession of extra-sensory perception by an animal might not always be of advantage to it unless this were direct knowledge counterbalanced by confirmatory and more precise messages reaching it from its special senses. Dr. Thouless drives this home to us by citing the difficult position in which a deer might be placed if it were entirely dependent for its safety on telepathic warnings of the approach of a tiger. 'It would be unable to decide whether the telepathic warning on this score referred to a tiger in the vicinity now, to one a hundred and fifty miles away, or to one that would be there tomorrow. And to this we have to add that if it were a deer conversant with the subtleties of Freudian symbolism, it could not even be sure whether the animal was a tiger at all and not a veiled intimation of some sex aggression.'

Evolution and Brain Development

As evolution progressed it began to move amongst the mammals in the direction of greater and greater brain development. This gave rise to the appearance of more and more intelligent animals with larger and larger brains and as the size of that organ increased the animal in question became much less dependent on the aid previously given by extra-sensory perception. According to Bergson, the brain has a very special function to perform. It is primarily a selective agent which focuses an animal's attention on the events in its environment which are of practical importance to it in the fierce struggle for survival. The brain also simplifies the picture of the outside world which the animal receives through its sense organs, so that it is able to deal with it in a more orderly fashion, bit by bit. Moncrieff, like Thouless, points to the confusion which might be produced in the unprotected animal by the arrival of a sudden flood of extra-sensory impressions from without. He looks upon an animal's visual, olfactory and auditory organs as being canalizing mechanisms by which an animal is saved from being overwhelmed by a flood of irrelevant ESP impressions.

Conclusions reached on the subject of Extra-Sensory Perception

Having examined carefully the foregoing evidence in favour and against the existence of another sense or senses beyond those which are known to us as the special senses, I think it is possible to summarize our conclusions as follows:

1. That this additional Sense, or Psi Factor, makes itself evident from time to time in man;

2. That the Psi Function in man is not so limited by questions of space and of time as are man's special senses;

3. That the various activities of man's Psi Function are in all probability governed by laws of their own which have not, as yet, been discovered;

4. That a *percept* of our special senses often provides a useful starting point for a Psi Function activity and that a sensory *percept* may also help us to bring to a focus data which have been received from the said activity of the Psi Function;

5. That a considerable, though as yet undetermined, number of people are partly motivated and conditioned by the Psi Function but that comparatively few of them are aware of this fact, for more often than not they are surprised and even disconcerted when the hidden factor of the Psi Function obtrudes itself on their notice.

7

The Divining Art

Divining is amongst the most ancient of the arts and it is still being practised in many parts of the world. In order to live effectively it is necessary to have foreknowledge and divining is amongst the methods by which man has attempted to obtain this. Sometimes the forecasting of the future has depended on the acuteness of man's perception and on his memory of what has happened in the past in similar circumstances. By such means the leaders of a tribe were able to recognize the conditions which were favourable to the planting of crops or to the undertaking of a hunting expedition. It was also of the greatest importance that the leaders of wandering tribes should be able to discover springs in what appeared to be waterless country and here water-divining was sometimes employed by those who possessed the capacity to use it. Men who were in possession of these superior powers became the wizards and the medicine men of the community.

The ability of the leaders of the tribe to find water usually depended on their past experience and on the acuteness of their special senses but the water-diviners made use of certain subliminal powers which they had developed in themselves to a high degree of efficiency. Which of the two methods was responsible for the discovery of water on any given occasion would be a difficult matter to decide, for the two factors of careful observation and of true water-divining would have often worked together. When shooting in East Africa in the year 1908, the writer of this book was frequently astonished by the capacity shown by the native leaders of his safari to discover water in what appeared, to him, to be waterless country. On being questioned about their methods they replied quite simply that they could 'smell' water, even when it was two or three miles away from them. But the term 'smell' may well have been the only word they could find for describing the intervention of some extra-sensory method of perception.

Water Divining

Water divining or 'dowsing' is only one aspect of the many-sided Psi faculty in man and what is true of water-dowsing is true also of the search for minerals and of the discovery of lost articles and people. The earliest mention of divining that I have been able to discover in English literature is in an illustrated article on this subject which was published in the year 1571. The illustration shows two expert metal diviners at work and the divining twigs in their hands are both pointing to an area of ground where two other men are already beginning to dig. In order that there may be no doubt in the reader's mind about the nature of the divining rods being used, a third dowser is depicted in the background securing for himself a new Y-shaped twig from a tree.

The art of divining for water and metals has been passed down through the centuries from generation to generation and it seems always to have been a particularly popular art in France. Divining has now been extended into many other fields than those of prospecting for water and minerals. In 1692 Pierre Garmier, a Montpellier physician wrote a treatise in which he claimed that the divining rod was an exceedingly useful instrument for all sorts of purposes including that of tracking down criminals. He recounted how a certain farm labourer in the Dauphiné district of France had so great a reputation for divining that he was asked to go to Lyons, where a dual murder had recently been committed, in the hope that he would be able to discover the murderer. The physician narrates that as soon as the diviner entered the cellar in which the killing had taken place, his divining rod began to swirl violently in his hand. Guided by its movements and going wherever it indicated he eventually traced the murderer down into the Southern part of France and finally came to a halt outside the Beaucaire jail. He made it known to the authorities therefore that the murderer was somewhere within this building and his statement was later proved to be entirely correct. After a re-examination of all the inmates of the prison, one of them confessed to having committed the crime.

Dowsing Methods in the Detection of Crime

Dowsing methods are still being employed for finding lost people and for tracking down criminals and many accounts of it used for these two purposes are to be found in *The Journal of the British Society of Dowsers*. The following is an example of the modern use of the pendulum – now used as a substitute for a twig by many dowsers – for the detection of crime. A few years before the outbreak of the last war, a bachelor, whom we shall call Mr. S., advertised for a housekeeper in a provincial Italian paper. The said bachelor lived alone in the village of Caslano, which lies on the shores of Lake Lugano. A young woman in Berne applied for the job, was accepted and was duly installed in Mr. S.'s house. A few weeks later her parents received a letter from Mr. S. in which he explained that their daughter did not quite meet his requirements as a housekeeper and that she was on her way home. He stated that he had just seen her off at the station, but that as she intended to break her journey and to stay somewhere with friends he was unable to tell them when she would arrive. He added that he had discovered the keys of her luggage in her bedroom after he had returned from the station, and that he was enclosing them in this letter.

When their daughter failed to turn up the anxious parents explained what had happened to the police and the only information the police could give them was to the effect that on several previous occasions Mr. S. had advertised for a housekeeper and that the police had never been able to establish contact with them subsequently. Having failed to get any satisfaction from the police, the alarmed parents appealed to a certain Mr. K. who had made for himself a great name in that locality as a radiesthetist. He agreed to help them. K. asked them for some piece of clothing from their daughter's luggage which had by now arrived, and also for the letter which S. had written to them. He likewise asked for any photographs which their daughter might possibly have taken and sent them, whilst she had been living at Caslano.

Having examined all these articles very carefully with his pendulum, K. made the following announcement. 'Your daughter is dead. She was probably strangled. Her body is in Lake Lugano at a depth of so many metres and at such a distance from S.'s house. He is her murderer.' The police had now been placed in a very difficult position for they possessed no evidence to support this view that the girl had been murdered. But K. was so confident of the truth of his statement that they agreed to act in conjunction with him. A few days later a car drew up at the door of S.'s house, from which alighted the Public Prosecutor posing as a lawyer, two stalwart plain clothes policemen and Mr. K., who was said to be a friend of the family's. On meeting S. they made various inquiries of him. 'What were the clothes his housekeeper was wearing on her departure? The date and the precise time of her departure?' Finally they asked whether or not she liked taking photographs at Caslano. To the last question S. replied in the affirmative and at this point K. took entire charge of the proceedings. He said: 'Look, I have here a few photographs sent to me by your housekeeper's anxious parents, photographs which I have examined in my own special manner. You tell me that you saw the girl off by the train to Lugano on Tuesday, 5 June. Are you sure that you are not mistaken, for, according to my radiesthetic examination, that does not seem to be possible.' But S. persisted in his assertion, so K., looking him straight in the face, said 'That is not correct, for according to my examination, the missing girl was no longer alive on Saturday, 2 June and by Tuesday, 5 June she had been deposited somewhere in the lake here in front of your garden.'

S. was now thrown into a state of dire confusion and losing control he hurled himself on K., so that he had to be secured. K. then continued thus: 'Here is a snap of the room in which she slept. Let us enter it and I will try to retrace, step by step, the course your victim took, not to the station, but to the lake.' When they had arrived in the bedroom, K. drew his pendulum out of his pocket. In his left hand he held the photo of the missing girl and in his right the pendulum, which he allowed to oscillate freely over one of S.'s hands. 'It was here' he said 'that you strangled your servant, on the night of Friday and the next night you dragged her body through the garden to a boat.' The story ends with the party, including S. leaving the house and getting into a boat in which had been stowed dragging tackle. K. stood on the bank of the lake and he allowed the pendulum to oscillate, taking up a certain direction which indicated that in which the body was lying in the water. This alignment was then marked by means of two stakes and a similar procedure was carried out at another point on the bank. K. now instructed the boatmen to row away from the bank 'until they had reached a point at which the two alignments could be sighted simultaneously . . . The boatmen . . . let down the grapnels and after several attempts a heavy object was gripped and raised to the surface. It proved to be a sack weighted with stones and containing also the body of S.'s victim.' The writer of the article ends by stating that the Public Prosecutor 'declared at a legal conference that without the co-operation of the Radiesthetist K. the crime would never have been discovered'.

Many questions were raised by this astonishing story. 'Could the statement of the Public Prosecutor be relied upon?' 'Did the radiesthetist K. actually play so great a part in the detection of the crime as he was credited with playing?' 'How could the movement of a pendulum reveal all these facts?' It is feasible only to return an answer to the last of these three questions, an answer which is admittedly incomplete. What part did the pendulum play in this drama? It was not responsible for the discovery of the truth. All that it did was to reveal what had been discovered by the radiesthetist's Subliminal Mind. Unconsciously perhaps, K. had put to his own mind a series of questions: 'Was the answer to this question "yes" or "no"?' And without any delay the pendulum had indicated the subliminal mind's answer by its manner of swinging. Then the next question was asked and answered by the movement of the pendulum in a similar manner. The truth might have been revealed by a different method— for example, by a flash of clairvoyance, or by automatic writing, but on this occasion, and for reasons of its own, Mr. K.'s Subliminal Mind preferred to express itself in terms of slight movements of his hand. The pendulum exaggerated and made evident these movements which otherwise might not have been noticed.[1]

The Scientific Investigation of Dowsing

What scientific evidence can be produced in support

[1] *Journal of the British Society of Dowsing*, vol. XI.

of the many claims which have been made by the practitioners of the ancient dowsing art? It has to be admitted straight away that less support of an experimental nature exists for water-dowsing and other forms of divining than for the other varieties of extra-sensory perceptions which have been discussed in this book. Systematic field-tests for water-divining are difficult to arrange and to carry out. They also necessitate a great deal of digging in order to discover whether the diviner's statements are correct or not. Moreover, water-diviners may be asked to work in conditions which are unfavourable to the manifestation of their powers. In consequence of all these difficulties the results of the dowsing tests have sometimes been disappointing. This was certainly true of the tests specially arranged by Dr. Gardner Murphy of the American Society for Psychical Research in 1950. On this occasion twenty-seven dowsers were submitted to a number of carefully controlled tests, the ground which had been chosen for this purpose being a flat sandy slope in Maine, where water was known to exist but at unknown depths. The twenty-seven competitors were asked to select the best sites at which to start digging and to state beforehand the depth at which water was likely to be found. Their scoring was no higher than could be accounted for by chance alone and it was lower than that of a water engineer who accompanied them on their rounds and who located water by ordinary commonsense water-prospecting methods.

Nevertheless, a great many striking successes have been obtained by individual dowsers who have been specially commissioned to prospect for water in dry countries. Major Pogson who, several years ago, was appointed official water-diviner to the Government of Bombay, fully justified his appointment, for only two out of the forty-nine wells dug at his orders failed to yield the quantity of water at the depth at which he had predicted that it would be found. What increases the impressiveness of Major Pogson's dowsing performance is the fact that the great majority of his wells were dug in drought-stricken areas, and on sites where previous diggings had proved unsuccessful. The majority of the underground springs he discovered were located in the Deccan which, from the geologist's point of view, is an unpromising country in which to discover water.

Dr. T. T. B. Watson, the President of the Medical Society for the Study of Radiesthesia, cites another outstanding success on the part of a water diviner. This success was scored during the First World War at a very critical moment in the Gallipoli campaign, when some of the British troops who had been landed on the peninsula were nearing exhaustion owing to the intense heat and to the absence of all water. Using a piece of bent copper wire as his divining rod, Sapper Kelly succeeded in discovering an underground spring which was situated within a hundred yards of Divisional Headquarters, a spring which provided 2,000 gallons of water every hour. Within a week he had located thirty-two other wells, thus providing sufficient water to satisfy the needs of 100,000 men, each man receiving a daily ration of a gallon. According to Dr. Watson the 'skilled dowser can not only locate the place where a

well should be sunk to find water; he can also predict
the depth, within a few feet, at which it will be found
and the yield in gallons an hour that will be delivered.
The figures are arrived at by some operators by
measuring the distances between the dowsing reaction
zones that are to be found over an underground
stream'.

The traditional instrument of the dowsers is a forked
hazel twig but any other resilient material can be used
for this purpose. The two free ends of the twig are
grasped by the hands of the diviner in such a way that
the instrument is in a very delicate state of equilibrium.
When the dowser comes into the neighbourhood of an
underground stream, the rod is twisted upwards or
downwards, the movement occurring spontaneously
and quite independently of the conscious will of the
dowser. Sometimes the movement is so strong that
diviners are unable to control the twig and it is broken
into pieces. The movement may be associated with
physical and psychological reactions on the part of the
dowser. Dr. Watson writes of 'tinglings in the arms and
legs, muscular contractions, giddiness and profuse
perspiration'.[1] Some dowsers even go into contortions
but as soon as they leave the vicinity of the water zone
all these physical and psychological phenomena
immediately cease. Cloudy and stormy weather is said
by some diviners to have an adverse effect on dowsing.

A careful examination of a dowser at work supports
the view that the sole purpose of the dowsing instrument, whatever form it takes, is to exaggerate and to
render more obvious, very small movements occurring

[1] T. T. B. Watson, *Radiesthesia and some Associated Phenomena.*

in the muscles of the dowser's arms. Colonel K. W. Merrylees, who has a great deal of experience in dowsing, writes of it as follows: 'To give an example, the traditional "V" twig is held in such a way that the end moves through a wide arc when the forearm muscles are very slightly contracted or extended. All these effects can be obtained by conscious muscular effort but the true dowsing indication appears to be a completely involuntary reflex movement. Some dowsers have thought that it was the instrument which was being moved by an outside force, and have favoured therefore, a purely physical explanation of dowsing'.[1] Colonel Merrylees adds the interesting statement that the small involuntary movements on which dowsing depends may be made by a person who possesses no dowsing experience at all, provided that he be lightly touched by a dowser when both are moving together over a line which the dowser has previously found 'to be the centre of a subsoil flow'.

The most serious objection to this idea that dowsing is due to the action of a physical force emanating from the regions of the hidden water is the success of the process known as 'map-dowsing'. In map-dowsing, which is often used as a preliminary to dowsing on the actual site, the dowser holds a pointer in one hand and a pendulum in the other hand and, aided by these two instruments, he may be able to trace on a large scale map the course taken by subsoil streams which are not marked on that map and of whose existence nobody has hitherto been aware. These streams may lie deep under the ground and they may be situated in a country of

[1] Colonel Merrylees, Private Communication.

whose geological nature and configuration the dowser knows nothing at all. Surely the success of map-dowsing indicates that dowsing is a *psychic* faculty and one of many activities of the region of the mind in which we are particularly interested, Myers's Subliminal Self. That distinguished scientist and member of the S.P.R., Sir William Barrett, supported the psychic explanation of dowsing a long time ago. He regarded all forms of divining as being manifestations of the working of the Extra-Sensory Perception faculty in man and everything which has been discovered since Sir William Barrett's time has tended to support this idea of his. Many additional observations can be marshalled in favour of it. For example, that well-known French authority on this subject, the Abbé Bouly, states that when he is engaged in dowsing he frequently receives a visual impression of an underground stream. So also does the English expert, John Pimms, claim that he often possesses knowledge of the situation in which water will later be found before he starts his actual dowsing.

All of the above facts support the view that the dowser is obtaining knowledge from a source which lies outside the realm of his special senses and beyond the reach of his reason. In order to make contact with this source it is necessary that he should be in what is known as a 'receptive state'. Colonel Merrylees writes of this state as follows: 'My own experience of dowsing is that it does not require concentration, in the ordinary sense of excluding things from one's thoughts, but rather a form of receptivity which may be induced by the formulation of the problem, usually by asking oneself the appropriate question and the taking up of the instrument either on the ground or over a map. When the right "drill" has been carried out, the receptivity remains until it is concluded by a conscious act, which usually includes disconnexion from the dowsing instrument. Whilst in this receptive state the ordinary acts of selecting a route on which to walk, or an arc on the map, talking to others present etc. can be carried on without interfering with the survey.'

As has previously been pointed out, dowsing methods are frequently used for purposes other than finding water. For example, Lucian Landau describes how on one occasion he placed in his pocket the oldest article he could find, an ancient coin, and set out across Exmoor with the express purpose of discovering some relics of prehistoric man. At the end of a three-mile walk he stopped, marked off a square foot of earth and with the help only of his hands he eventually disinterred from the loose earth a prehistoric arrowhead. The coin in his pocket had acted as a 'directive', that is to say, it had helped him to hold in his mind a clear picture of something made by man very long ago. Similarly those who prospect for oil, or for gold, may carry on their persons a small bottle of oil or a gold coin. Not that this is entirely necessary, for the words 'gold' or 'oil' plainly written on a scrap of paper or, when searching for a missing person, some article which has previously belonged to that person will act as a 'directive'. In the opinion of Colonel Merrylees the only limits to the use of dowsing methods are the limits which are imposed by the dowser's own mind and personality. He may eventually be able to reduce still further the restrictions in his dowsing capacity, or they may prove too formidable to be removed. 'Whatever special line a dowser may seek to follow, water, minerals, missing people or diseases and treatment, none will surely succeed unless he or she possesses sensitivity of mind, experience and confidence.'

All of these facts about dowsing makes it almost certain that dowsing is a manifestation of that faculty of the Unconscious Mind to which the name Psi faculty has been given. That it is a faculty which primitive man possessed and that we all have it in a greater or a lesser degree is also certain. This being so dowsing should be regarded as being an entirely natural gift and a gift which modern man is more likely to be in process of losing than of developing. It may even be true that primitive man possessed this extra-sensory faculty in a higher degree than we moderns possess it. It is also possible that extra-sensory perception may play a part in the behaviour of animals.

If we watch the manœuvring of a flock of starlings as a single unit in the air, and if we bear in mind the astonishing ability of very young birds, in their first season, to act as an advance party in the annual migration, it is difficult to avoid coming to the conclusion that some force of a clairvoyant nature is helping them to co-ordinate their behaviour. The same is true of that astonishing phenomena the annual emigration westward of European eels and of the counter movement Eastward of American eels. At a certain time of the year all the European eels desert their customary haunts in European rivers and set out courageously for an unknown destination in the

Caribbean Sea. At the same time there is a corresponding Eastward movement of American eels towards the European shores of the Atlantic. We can call this 'instinct' if we like to do so, but the mere coining of a word does not provide us with a satisfactory explanation of what is happening. We are encouraged by these remarkable events to postulate the existence of some directive force of an extra-sensory nature and as Moncrieff has pointed out, the behaviour of the 'individuals who make up certain insect communities points still more strongly to the existence in insects of some extra-sensory faculty. The multifarious communal activities of termites, ants, bees and wasps, to which every individual is so admirably adapted, and the activities so well adjusted to the needs of the *whole* community are difficult to explain without its help.'[1] Anyone who has kept bees and who has watched their activities in an observation hive will agree with Moncrieff that there exists not only an astonishingly intimate relationship between the myriads of individuals of the hive but also some central controlling force as well.

When we come to the white ants or termites of South Africa the need for some binding force of this kind, or for the existence of some form of group-mind, becomes almost imperative. It has to be remembered that the specialized forms of termites, such as the soldiers and the workers, have this in common, that they are entirely devoid of the sense organs of sight and sound, and yet, blind and deaf though they be, they carry on, with the

[1] M. M. Moncrieff, *The Clairvoyant Theory of Perception.*

greatest efficiency, their highly specialized work within the vast network of underground passages of the termitary. Their ability to do all this is particularly astonishing when we bear in mind the fact that termitaries may extend underground over an area of a hundred square yards. This was the problem to which Marais, the author of the *Soul of the White Ant*, devoted a great deal of thought and after many years of patient study of it, he came to the conclusion that the source of the mysterious co-ordinating force within the termitary was the *body of the queen*. After her nuptial flight, the queen remains, for the rest of her life, imprisoned within a cell situated in the centre of the ant-heap. She is the termitary's captive and in some unknown way she appears to be acting also as its brain. Marais writes that each individual 'forms part of a separate organism of which the queen is the psychological centre. The queen has the power, call it instinct if you will, of influencing the workers and soldiers in a certain way which enables them to perform collective duties . . . As soon as the queen is destroyed all the instincts of the workers and soldiers cease immediately'.

We stand in the presence of a riddle here to which no one as yet has returned a satisfactory answer. Perhaps Bergson has approached as near to an explanation as anybody when he declares that: 'Instinct is sympathy. If this instinct could extend its object and also reflect upon itself, it would give us the key to vital operations – just as intelligence, developed and disciplined, guides us into matter. For, intelligence and instinct are turned in opposite directions, the former towards inert matter, the latter towards life. Intelligence . . . will deliver up to us more and more completely the secret of physical operations . . . It goes all round life, taking from outside the greatest possible number of views of it, drawing it into itself instead of entering into it . . . But it is to the very inwardness of life that intuition leads us – by intuition I mean instinct that has become disinterested, self-conscious, capable of reflecting upon its object and of enlarging it indefinitely.'[1] To attempt to add anything to Bergson's masterly handling of the problem would be to spoil what he has written.

[1] Henri Bergson, *Creative Evolution*.

8

Radiesthesia and Radionics

The methods used in water-divining are now being applied over a very wide field of practice which include the diagnosis and the treatment of illness. In this chapter the diagnosis and treatment of illness by means of Radiesthesia and Radionics will be described. The literal meaning of the word 'Radiesthesia' is 'sensitivity to radiations' and the word 'Radionics' is now being used by many people to denote the branch of radiesthesia in which the simple instruments of the water-diviner and of the practitioner of radiesthesia are being replaced by elaborate instruments of various kinds. Practitioners of Radiesthesia and Radionics usually have a different attitude to illness to that of the allopathic doctor, an attitude which is more closely allied to that of followers of the Homeopathic school of Medicine. They regard diseases as being the result of a general disharmony in the functioning of a living organism, a disharmony which is often due to the impact of some hostile force. The symptoms of the disease are the more obvious signs of the general derangement of functions which has taken place in the organism, and treatment entails an effort on the part of the practitioner to re-establish the harmony which has been lost.

Certain changes in technique were necessary in order to render water-divining methods suitable for the detection and treatment of illness and the first alteration was the substitution of a pendulum for the water-dowser's forked twig. The Catholic priests of France, and particularly the Abbé Bouly, Curé of Hardelot, were leaders in this new movement. They have greatly extended the use of the pendulum and have applied it to the solving of a great many different kinds of problems. For example, the Abbé Bouly claimed that a pendulum could be used to estimate the percentage of salts present in a given sample of water by holding in one hand samples of known quantities of salts and in the other hand the pendulum. The same method was applied to the testing of water for various forms of bacterial contamination. The pendulum analysis of water has been followed by the detection of infections in the human body and also in the bodies of animals by the same methods. The pendulum is also employed both for selecting the appropriate remedy and for estimating the dosage required.

Journals dealing with the new art of radiesthesia soon began to appear in different countries and in these journals such subjects as the best design for a pendulum and the best way of using it were discussed. As a result of all this publicity the use of the pendulum for the detection and the treatment of diseases has spread rapidly, more especially on the Continent. As had happened previously in water-dowsing, many of the pendulum users stated that they were aware of sensations in their hands, and this has led to some of them dispensing with their pendulums and relying for guidance on sensations alone. The late Dr. Dudley Wright, who first forsook the profession of surgeon in order to become a physician and subsequently adopted radiesthetic methods of treatment, is an example of a radiesthetist who relied solely on the sensations he felt in his hands.

Before proceeding any further it is advisable that the author should make clear to his readers his own attitude to the diagnosis and treatment of illness by the methods about to be described. The attitude he is endeavouring to maintain is that of the impartial observer. He has no personal experience of any of these unorthodox methods of diagnosis and treatment and all that he has attempted to do has been to obtain information from the practitioners of these arts whom he has happened to meet. Some of them have been well qualified and highly responsible medical men who, as the result of their careful trial in these methods, are now fully convinced of their value. It is difficult therefore for the author to regard their verdicts as of no account. So also is it difficult for him to attribute the rapid spread of radiesthetic methods of treatment in the various countries of Western Europe – and particularly in France – to imagination and to the vagaries of medical fashion. Naturally he can offer no personal guarantee of the value of these unorthodox methods of diagnosis and treatment but he believes them to be worthy of investigation. If he had written a book on the Unconscious Mind without ever having mentioned the application of the divining art to the diagnosis and treatment of illness he would have been guilty of a serious omission.

The Treatment of Illnesses

Dr. Westlake, a practitioner in radiesthetic methods,

describes his method of healing illness under two headings. He writes: 'The general field of therapeutics can be divided into two main divisions – The Analytic and the Unitary. In the first falls most of modern medicine. Here the technique is essentially analytical; the whole endeavour is to arrive at accurate diagnosis, i.e. to ascertain what parts of the organism are at fault and the factors, chemicals, microbes, etc. which have produced these pathological conditions and then to treat these specific causes and the diseased organs or tissues. The larger part of radiesthetic technique and practice also falls into this category, whether by pendulum or instrumental. Its superiority to the more orthodox methods I think we would claim to lie in more accurate and subtle pin-pointing of the patho-logical conditions, and particularly, of the underlying causes, seldom arrived at by the ordinary methods of diagnosis . . . The great disadvantage of the Analytic method is that, as illustrated by modern medicine, it tends to specialization. One tends to think in parts instead of wholes; one is dealing not with a person who is sick but with a heart case, a liver case, a lung case and so on. An exception to this is Dr. McDonagh's conceptions which relate all parts to the whole, as summed up in his dictum, "There is only one disease!" '

Dr. Westlake's second or *Unitary* category of thera-peutics comes of a very ancient lineage. In it an exact diagnosis is comparatively unimportant. The practi-tioner of Unitary medicine is dealing with a whole, with a sick *person*, who is out of harmony, physically, mentally, psychically or spiritually, and the object of therapy is to restore to him what he has lost. This being so the therapeutic agent is of a general nature and is closely allied both to spiritual healing and to the method known as the 'laying on of hands'. But Westlake agrees that in actual practice it is often desirable to combine the two categories of therapeutics, the Analytic and the Unitary. Many practitioners of radiesthesia also make use of some form of broadcasting apparatus, for although they lay chief emphasis on the psychic factor in their treatment they are of the opinion that broadcasting on the right wave-length is also helpful to the patient.

The Treatment of Absent Patients

The majority of radiesthesia practitioners prefer to have their patients present in person, both for diagnosis and for treatment, but if need be, the presence of the patient can be dispensed with. Should a diagnosis have to be made and treatment given in the absence of the patient, some link with him is desirable and here the radiesthesia practitioner resorts to a principle which was of great importance in the ancient practice of 'sympathetic' magic. According to the medieval magicians and according also to the witch-doctors of today, that which has once formed a part of a whole still remains linked with the whole even when it has been removed from it. For this reason the witch-doctor of today usually asks for something belonging to the individual on whom he is required to practise magic, some paring from his nails, a fragment of discarded food, or some article of his clothing. Possessed of one or other of these articles he has a link with the individual which is said to give him greater power over him.

In a similar way, the practitioner of radiesthesia, or of radionics, makes use of a drop of the absent patient's blood, or of his saliva, in order to preserve this connexion with him. It is true that the expert in radionics tunes into the 'wave length' or the frequency of this drop of blood by turning the vulcanite knobs of an elaborate machine but the principle is still the same as the principle which was formerly used in ancient sympathetic magic. So also has this method of diagnosing illness much in common with the particular form of extra-sensory perception known as Psychometry, that is to say, the art of obtaining knowledge by holding in the hand some article belonging to a person who may be entirely unknown to the clairvoyant. Those who are capable of this form of extra-sensory perception will often reveal facts about the owner of the article of an astonishingly exact nature and a good example of this will be given in chapter eleven.

The Nature of the Forces involved in Illness

Beliefs concerning the nature of the forces which have been disturbed by illness have changed in different ages and usually they are in accordance with contemporary scientific theories. For example, in the second half of the eighteenth century, Mesmer, who may be regarded as being one of the pioneers of the Unitary method of treating illness, believed that the forces which had been disturbed in his patients were forces of a magnetic nature. This explains why, in the earlier years of his practice, he made considerable use of magnets in treating his patients. When a young man, Mesmer had met a Jesuit priest who was also an astronomer and this priest had taught him that the energy of magnetism pervaded the whole of space and linked together, in a single system, not only the heavenly bodies, but also all creatures living on the surface of the earth. The teaching of this priest and his method of treating illnesses with magnets made a great impression on the young Mesmer and at a later date he began to make use of the priest's methods himself. But his critics – and they were many – poked fun at his magnets and in the later years of his practice, he wrote a book entitled *Memoire sur le Decouverte du Magnetism Animal*. In it he made it clear to the world that he regarded the use of magnets as being only a subsidiary form of treatment. He wrote: 'The physician and doctors with whom I have been in correspondence . . . have taken upon themselves to spread about either that the magnet was the only means I employed or that I used electricity as well . . . The desire to refute such errors, once and for all, and to do justice to truth, determined me to make no further use of electricity or the magnet from 1776 onwards.' He also pointed out in his book that although '*animal* magnetism' had much in common with what he calls *mineral* magnetism they were not identical forces. Yet in spite of the difference between the animal and the mineral form of magnetism the former could 'be communicated to other animals and to inanimate bodies'. He wrote: 'Its action is exerted at a distance, without the aid of an intermediate body and it may be stored up, concentrated and transported.' Mesmer likewise states in his writings that 'all animate bodies are not equally susceptible; there are some, although very few, whose properties are so opposed that their very presence destroys all the effect of magnetism in other bodies'. It was along the lines of 'non-susceptibility to magnetism' that Mesmer explained the fluctuations in the success of his treatment by means of animal magnetism, just as in modern times fluctuation in the success of radiesthetic and radionic forms of treatment is occasionally explained by radiesthesia experts in terms of incorrect wavelengths.

Whether we regard Mesmer as a charlatan or as a genius, the fact remains that he obtained a great many cures and also exerted a salutary effect on the development of medicine. He complained, and with good reason, that the doctors of his day looked only at the *physical* aspects of illness and completely neglected other aspects of it, and more particularly, the effect of the illness on the patient's mind. And there can be no doubt of the benefit conferred by this broader outlook of Mesmer's on his treatment of patients and disease. His successes were so apparent to everybody that King Louis was moved to appoint a Royal Commission to investigate Mesmer's methods of treatment. The report subsequently issued by the Commission agreed that Mesmer had obtained many remarkable cures by his methods, but it threw considerable doubt on the existence of such a thing as 'animal magnetism'. A committee of medical men sifting the same material as that examined by King Louis's Commission would probably come to a similar conclusion today, namely that the implicit faith of Mesmer's patients in his capacity to cure them was an important factor in his successes. But it is almost certain that there were other healing factors in his treatment in addition to the factor of suggestion. Mesmer himself was convinced that he had found the right way of manipulating the essential and vital energies within man and of mobilizing them for the purposes of cure, and he may not have been entirely wrong in arriving at this conclusion. The term Animal Magnetism has disappeared from medicine and has been replaced by the more up-to-date words 'radiesthesia', 'radionics' and 'wave length', but the principles on which Mesmer's methods were based are very similar to those on which the modern practices of radiesthesia and radionics are based.

Reichenbach's Ideas on the Subject

Reichenbach followed closely on the heels of Mesmer. He was an eminent chemist and he had been deeply influenced by Mesmer's methods, even though he was unable to accept the theory that all living bodies were pervaded by an energy called 'animal magnetism'. In order to study what the forces in the human body actually were, Reichenbach brought together a number of people who had claimed to be particularly sensitive to 'animal magnetism' and, with their help, he carried out a number of experiments. He started by taking special precautions to prevent his subjects from influencing each other by previously talking together and he then asked each of them separately and privately what he or she meant by the term 'animal magnetism'. He found that there was a general basis of agreement between them on this rather obscure subject of 'magnetism'. For example, many of them stated that they became aware of 'red flames and a feeling of warmth' emanating from the *positive* arm of a horse-shoe magnet and of blue flames, giving a cool sensation, emanating from its negative arm. They also added that the flames could be sent by blowing on them, as happened when one blew on a candle flame. Reichenbach gave the new name *Odyl* to the energy which Mesmer had called 'animal magnetism' and like Mesmer he regarded it as a cosmic energy which existed everywhere in the universe, but unequally distributed so that it tended to flow from one concentration of it to another concentration of it. He had changed the name of the cosmic force but his *Odyl* possessed all of the characteristics of Mesmer's force 'animal magnetism'. The idea of a universal cosmic force had of course existed long before Mesmer, for both Paracelsus and Robert Fludd, a Rosicrucian writer of the seventeenth century, had written that this force entered into the structure of man as well as into the structure of the universe. Man was indeed a small scale model of the universe in which he lived, 'a microcosm in a microcosm'. 'He containeth in himself his heaven, circles, poles and stars, even as the great world outside . . . From the stars, the human body and all substances in the universe there radiates forth beams which reciprocally affect all other bodies.' For Fludd, as for many others of the older philosophers, man was 'a microcosm in a microcosm', constructed out of the same elements and permeated by the same energies which flowed through the rest of the universe. Up to the end of the eighteenth century theories of this kind were part of a religious system of thought which proclaimed that man was linked with the heavens as well as with the earth and that, this being so, the aim of man's life should be to be ruled by the higher elements in his nature rather than by its lower elements. In order to achieve this aim, man should submit himself continually to the Divine Will. But unwittingly Mesmer severed the close connexion between the idea of an all pervading energy and of man's submission to the Will of the Diety, so that the spiritual side of this ancient philosophy disappeared from it for good.

Radiesthesia and Radionics

The radiesthetic and radionic practitioners of today also picture the universe as being filled with an all-pervading energy in which all living things are immersed and like Mesmer and Reichenbach, they look upon their treatment as a means of restoring to their patients some of the energy which they have lost. But before describing their methods of treatment, something must be said about an earlier event in the radiesthesia movement which paved the way for what was to happen later. I am referring to the well-known work of Dr. Albert Abrams.

The Abrams Box

Albert Abrams was the son of a successful San Francisco business man and having inherited a considerable fortune, he was able to devote himself entirely to what interested him more than anything else in life – medical research. After graduating at Heidelberg, he returned to California and was elected to the Chair of Pathology at Stanford University. At that time the physicists were making spectacular progress in splitting the atom, hitherto regarded as being an indivisible and basic unit of matter, and this feat brought about a revolution in what, up to then, had been accepted as an entirely satisfactory notion of matter. Dr. Abrams was deeply impressed by the discoveries being made in physics and he believed that they had an important bearing on the science of medicine. The physicists had shown that 'matter' and 'energy' were interchangeable terms and also that matter was made up of minute parcels of positive and negative electricity called Protons and Electrons. The body being composed of matter and matter and energy being interchangeable terms man could be looked upon as being a 'field of energies', of an electrical nature. In a paper written for a medical journal, Dr. Abrams wrote: 'As physicians we dare not stand aloof from the recent amazing advances made by Physical Science. We cannot segregate the human body entirely from the other entities of the physical universe. Whether the object of our differentiation is a healthy man, or merely a mass of diseased tissues, we are, in either case, dealing only with a congregation of vibrant atoms which in their innumerable molecular combinations are the basic constituents of everything that exists.'

This statement was fully justified, but what was not logically justified was Abrams's subsequent inference that because atoms and molecules were now regarded as being electrical entities, diseases must necessarily be due to 'obscure electrical deviations of these molecules from the normal'. It is one thing to declare that the ultimate constituents out of which man is made are electrical units, and it is quite another thing to state categorically that the vibrant electrons which form a cancerous molecule are 'differently numbered and differently arranged from those forming a tuberculous molecule . . . and that the waves of radiations they send out would also be different and characteristic'.[1] The atoms of the cancerous molecule may be differently numbered and arranged and they may possibly emit different forms of radiations from the molecules of healthy tissues but there is no means of deciding whether this be true or not.

Dr. Eric Perkins has been kind enough to provide me with an account of Dr. Abrams's method of using a healthy body as a delicate instrument by means of which electrical disturbances can be detected and several years ago he gave me a practical demonstration of how this is done. Abrams's theory is that if pathological material from a sick patient be brought into contact with the body of a healthy subject, a change is produced in the percussion note obtained from different areas of the healthy subject's abdomen. Abrams was probably the first to make use of a *healthy* human body as an instrument by which to demonstrate the existence of certain electrical changes in an *unhealthy* body much in the same way that Galvani made use of muscle-nerve preparations taken from a frog, for the purpose of demonstrating the presence of electricity. He was also the first man to substitute a sub-atomic for a cellular theory of disease but whether or not he was justified in doing all this is an entirely different problem.

All that need be said here about Dr. Abrams's work is that the discoveries in physics focused his attention on what he regarded as being the electrical and sub-atomic manifestations of disease. At first he demon-

[1] From a lecture to the Society of Radiesthesia by Dr. Eric Perkins.

strated the existence of disease by placing a small fragment of material taken from a sick person on the forehead of the healthy subject, but at a later date this material was laid on one of two metal discs soldered to the ends of six feet of copper wire. The other metal disc was placed on the healthy subject's forehead and his abdomen was then lightly percussed in order to discover whether any change had taken place in percussion notes obtained in different areas of it, changes which could be attributed to reflex spasms in the abdominal muscles. The next improvement he made in his technique was the addition to the apparatus of a rheostat. The six feet of flex was divided and one of the cut ends was screwed into the 'input' terminal of the rheostat and the other into its 'output' terminal. This meant that the rheostat functioned much as a wireless set functions when we turn the knob in order to tune into wave lengths of different frequencies. According to a note added by the maker of this apparatus, John Bell & Croydon, 'the Abrams's rheostat was wound in such a manner as to be inductive and therefore variations in resistance would also cause variations in inductance. It is possible that the function of inductance was to pick up certain frequencies that Dr. Abrams had found to serve his special purposes.'[1] The final step in the development of the Abrams's methods was to substitute for a fragment of pathological tissue, a drop of the patient's blood. Abrams satisfied himself that a drop of blood on a piece of filter paper placed on one of the discs attached to the refloxophone

[1] Quoted by Dr. Perkins in *New Methods of Medical Diagnosis and Treatment*.

elicited the same neuro-muscular reactions in the healthy subject's abdominal muscles as those produced by actual contact with pathological material.

The above is a much shortened account of the instrument which afterwards became known as the 'Abrams Box' or the 'Magic Box'. Dr. Eric Perkins is of the opinion that this name was deliberately coined by Abrams's opponents in order to bring ridicule on his instrument and his methods, but I do not think that is necessarily the case for such an explanation is entirely superfluous. It was quite natural that the medical profession should be extremely dubious of the value of Abrams's indirect method of arriving at a medical diagnosis and that it should dismiss his apparatus as 'a bag of tricks' or as a 'magical box'. The magical is something to which a rational explanation cannot be given and Abrams's methods were far too mysterious to be explicable along acceptable scientific lines.

In 1924 a special Commission under the direction of Lord Horder was appointed to investigate the claims made by Dr. Abrams and his followers, but unfortunately it got no further than the issuing of the following unexpected and laconic statement: 'The fundamental proposition of Dr. Abrams is established to a very high degree.' It was a surprising preliminary to an official document and it is to be regretted that it had no sequel for it leaves us very much in the dark as to what the Commission really thought of Abrams's methods.

Radionics

Radionics may be looked upon as being a development of the divining art along instrumental as opposed to psychic lines. Whereas the practitioner of radies-thesia requires no apparatus more complicated than a pendulum or a simple form of broadcasting instrument, the practitioners of radionics place their faith in more and more elaborate instruments. These diagnostic instruments are not unlike the instrument originated by Dr. Abrams and one of the first to be devised – if not the first – was the Ruth Drown instrument. This instrument was modified at a later date by Mr. Delawarr of Oxford. The technique employed with both of these instruments was very similar, the first requirement being that the operator should determine what may be called the energy output of the organ or tissue to be tested. This the operator does by stroking a thin sheet of rubber stretched over a metal plate, a device which is called the detector unit. The patient is 'linked' to the instrument by means of a drop of blood, or saliva, there being no need for his presence at the examination. A 'rate' has been allotted to each of the organs and tissues of the body, both in health and disease, and also to a number of different entities such as bacteria, viruses, chemicals and hormones but the allotted rates bear no relationship to any known form of physical vibration. In making a diagnosis, the organ rates are set up in turn on the dials, the energy output being determined by stroking the rubber pad with the fingers and noting the moment at which the rubber becomes 'sticky' to it. To discover the nature of the pathological condition of the organ, the various disease rates are set up on the dials and it is claimed that by these means a complete record of the mental and physical state of the patient can be obtained.

Whatever may be the truth about these elaborate instruments used in radionics there can be no doubt that the *mind* of the operator plays a dominant part in the results obtained from them. This is shown by the fact that some operators appear to obtain positive and others only negative results from them, and to such an extent, that many people are now coming to the conclusion that the instrument merely acts as an aid or as a guide to the *psychic* factors in the Unconscious Mind of the operator. As the clairvoyant sometimes uses a crystal for the purpose of anchoring his attention, as the soothsayers of an earlier age gazed at the entrails of a recently slain animal, so does the clairvoyant practitioner in this Age of Science require for a similar purpose an elaborate piece of machinery. Customs alter but fundamentally the human *psyche* remains the same. If I were to go to Africa in order to make a documentary film of the methods of the African witch-doctor, I should expect him to arrive at my headquarters carrying with him a skull, a dried snake skin or two, a mask and a few herbs. In twentieth-century England, I should expect this paraphernalia to be replaced by an intricate piece of machinery.

At least two types of 'camera' have been devised and the makers of these instruments have claimed that with their help photographs of disease can be obtained from patients who are many miles distant, the only link with the patients being a spot of blood lying on the top of the instrument. The first of these cameras was the Drown instrument already mentioned, an instrument investigated by an independent scientific body which failed to substantiate the claims made for it. The

second camera to appear was the Delawarr Instrument.
As yet this camera has not been investigated by any
independent scientific authority and this being so all
that can be said about it with any certainty is that when
the films are handled by a certain sensitive expert at
the Delawarr Laboratories they may give positive
results, but when not so handled the results are likely
to be negative. It is quite possible that the photographs
said to have been obtained from the camera have an
entirely different origin from that which they are
supposed to have. Delawarr has himself stated that
the human mind is capable of exerting an action on a
sensitive photographic film and he has published
reproductions of 'thought-photographs' obtained in
this way.[1] He has also reproduced in his journal, *Mind
and Matter* reproductions of 'thought forms' produced,
in a similar way, in Japan. It is possible therefore that
the photographs said to have been obtained through
the agency of the camera are actually photographs of
ideas existing in the mind of the operator of the camera,
rather than pictures of diseases in distant patients.
Support for this view is provided by the fact that in my
opinion there is something slightly wrong with all of
the Delawarr photographs of diseased organs which
I have as yet seen. For example, the photograph of the
human intestines which was exhibited at a special
meeting at Oxford in the summer of 1959 is the
photograph of the sort of human intestines that a
layman, rather than a surgeon, would have visualized.
The photograph is realistic, but it is not realistic enough
to be convincing to a person as familiar with the

[1] See *Clairvoyance and Photography*, by T. Fukeri.

appearance of the human intestines as is an abdominal surgeon. This, taken in conjunction with the fact that the de la Warr films have to be rendered 'sensitive' by contact with one of the workers in the Delawarr Laboratories, makes it necessary to pause and think before accepting as satisfactory the official explanation of the origin of these photographs. The late Lord Horder was interested in the photographs produced by the Delawarr Camera and I can remember sitting in his garden near Petersfield discussing them with him. 'What is Delawarr actually photographing?' he asked me, and I answered that he claimed to be photographing diseased structure in distant patients. If I were to be asked this same question now I should answer quite differently. I should say, 'If you want my opinion, I should guess that he is photographing a visualization of a diseased structure in the mind of his assistant'. But this is only a guess for there is little on which to base any opinion. The camera, its mode of working and its products have never been examined and properly tested by any competent and *independent* authority.

Healing by the Laying on of Hands and by Spiritual Means
Of late there has been so great an increase in the use of what have been called spiritual methods of treatment that a few years ago the Archbishop of Canterbury appointed a special committee to investigate the matter. The author of this book was invited to appear before the committee, but not being an expert on this subject, he declined the invitation. The conclusions reached by the Committee were of a very vague and uncertain nature, for so many unknown quantities are involved

in the cure of illness that it is difficult or impossible to make any dogmatic statement on the subject. All that can really be said with any confidence, is that remarkable results may follow the use of what can only be called spiritual methods of treatment, and I am including under this heading radiesthetic methods as well as treatment by prayer and by the laying on of hands, or what in Mesmer's day would have been called the use of magical passes.

The Laying on of Hands

In the summer of 1959 I had the opportunity of watching the methods employed by a well-known healer of this kind, living in Florence, Dr. Francisco Racanelli. Dr. Racanelli has an international reputation and patients arrive at his house in Florence from many different countries in Europe, America and Asia. He has given the name Bio-radiant treatment to his method of healing patients and he has had astonishing successes with it. For him, as for Mesmer and for Reichenbach, the human individual is a transmitting and a receiving centre capable of being influenced by forces coming from other human centres, and he uses his hands as the best means of transmitting 'bio-radiant' energy from himself to his patients. He also claims to be highly sensitive to the different forms of radiation which reach him from his patients and from other people.

I have watched him at work. He is a man possessed of immense reserves of vital energy and he quickly obtains the confidence of his patients. But he denies that suggestion plays an important part in his treatment. He regards the confidence of his patient as being helpful to treatment but in no way essential to a cure, for he has had many successes with very young children, and also with animals, and such patients as these are not highly amenable to suggestion. He starts by teaching his anxious patients how to relax and how to obtain 'inner quiet' as they are lying there on his couch. He then places a hand anywhere from ten centimetres to thirty centimetres above the level of the inflamed or painful area and moves it slowly in one or other direction, and usually along the axis of the limb or the body. The first sensation of which the patient is likely to become aware as Racanelli's hand moves is a tingling sensation of variable intensity. This travels with the movement of his hand and it is often followed by a feeling of warmth. This sensation is not confined to the surface of the patient's body but penetrates into deeper regions and leads to a pleasing relaxed feeling. Although I did not question Dr. Racanelli on this subject, personally I have no doubt that the patient's sensation of warmth and comfort is due to the relaxing of his taut muscles, and to the dilation of many constricted blood vessels, in the affected area. Dr. Racanelli is a true exponent of psycho-somatic medicine and he pays as much attention to dealing with his patients' psychological problems as he does to healing them with his hands. I have very little doubt that Mesmer made similar 'magic' passes and for the same purposes that Racanelli does as his hands move slowly above the level of his patient's body. It is quite possible that some form of energy is thereby transferred from him to his patient, and whether that energy be spoken of in terms of magnetism, *odyl*, *prana* or *bio-radiant* energy, is a matter of very little importance. I am able to make only two more statements as the result of watching Dr. Racanelli at work. The first is that the 'tingling' and the subsequent 'warmth' felt by the patient was not the result of any previous suggestion, for Racanelli makes a point of never talking beforehand about what the patient is likely to feel as he moves his hand. The second observation is that the patient usually feels immediate benefit (it may of course only be temporary) from his treatment.

Spiritual Healing

At one time the priest and the physician were one. This was so in the early days of the Church and there is a passage in St. James's Epistle which proclaims that healing was part of the disciples' routine work. 'Is any among you suffering? Let him pray. Is any cheerful? Let him sing praise. Is any among you sick? Let him call for the elders of the Church; and let them pray over him, anointing him with oil in the name of the Lord; and the prayer of faith shall save him that is sick, and the Lord shall raise him up; and if he have committed sins it shall be forgiven him. Confess therefore your sins, one to another, and pray one to another, that ye may be healed. The supplication of a righteous man availeth much in its working.'[1]

But in course of time man was divided up by theologians and other thinkers into three separate entities, body, mind and spirit and to each part of man was allotted a different variety of specialist. The physician took charge of man's body, the psychiatrist

[1] James, vols. 13–16.

looked after the sick mind and the third component of man, the spirit, remained, as before, in the keeping of the priest. The great age of specialization began in this way.

Man cannot be summarily divided up in this fashion as though he were made of three separate entities which in some inexplicable way manage to react on one another. When a man becomes ill he must be treated as a whole, a fact which was implied by the writers of the Gospels when they said of a sick man 'that his faith hath made him whole'. It is a truth which is now being recognized more and more by the medical profession, for we doctors no longer divide illnesses up into physical and psychogenic or psychological illnesses. We now recognize the fact that it is seldom possible to make any sharp division of this kind between the various forms of illnesses we are called upon to treat. All that we can really say about an illness is that in this particular patient physical factors seem to predominate over psychological factors, and that in this other patient psychological factors seem to be the more important. What has always to be kept in mind is that the patient must be treated as a *whole* for a doctor is dealing, not with an illness or disease, but with a *man*.

Although doctors have fully recognized the importance of the psychological factors in illness and although they frequently call in the help of the psychologist they seldom enlist the aid of the specialist in disorders of the third or spiritual component of man. Lord Horder drew attention to this lack of co-operation between the doctor and the priest in an address entitled, 'Medicine and Religion', delivered at the Philosophical Institute of Edinburgh in 1938. He said: 'It is clear that there is a very definite point of contact between medicine and religion. For the whole man, and not merely a part of him, is concerned, or may be, in medicine, whether this be preventive or curative, and this *whole* includes his spirituality or religious temperament.'[1]

To have a religion is to have a certain attitude to life and also a manner of living, of which we frequently fall short but which is there all the time for our guidance. A religious person is consequently in a far happier and more satisfactory state than a man or woman who has no plan for living and whose life appears to be entirely without any meaning. Leslie Weatherhead gives an excellent account of this in his book *Psychology, Religion and Healing*. He quotes the case of a doctor who describes how the spiritual conflict within himself, which prevented him from ever being completely at peace, manifested itself physically in an obscure septic condition. The doctor's description of his own illness continues as follows: 'Happily my adviser combined a sound knowledge of physical medicine with a keen insight into the non-physical problems of health. He told me that it was unlikely that physical troubles were at the bottom of my illness, and suggested that in my way of life and in my attitude towards life might be found the source of my troubles. Little by little I began to see myself as I was. Self-centred, anxious about many things, a tangle of conflicting and incompatible purposes. "On a sunny November morning I was descending a hillside when I was aware – with deep emotion – that a clean cut must be made with the past.

[1] *Fortnightly Review*, October 1938.

I must cease striving for my own ends and purposes, must cheerfully embrace whatever plans or purposes God might have for me; must be prepared to be well or ill; must subject my hitherto dominant self to the one purpose of the Lord of Life for me. As I did so, a deep Peace followed and spread to Joy. For inward strife and chaos were given Peace and Joy. At such times we experience a lightness of heart, an adventurous abandon, which he who calculates chances in the lottery of life can never know nor comprehend. From this time on my physical health steadily improved." '

Dr. Howard Collier, author of *Modern Theory and Practice of Healing*, makes the following comment on the above. 'Here we find, I am persuaded, the essential living core of Spiritual Healing. It arises from the glad submission of the self as a whole, and as a personality, to the Will of God for us. To heal is to make whole; to be healed is to be made whole. It was in this manner that the Healer came to me.'

9

Apparitions

'Do you believe in Ghosts?' This was a question particularly appropriate to Christmas time when sitting with friends round a log fire, roasting chestnuts, or perhaps only watching the ballet-dance of the flames amongst the logs. And more often than not the inquiry elicited the story of the well-known ghost that inhabited some old Scottish castle or was followed by a description of a 'Grey Lady' who haunted the garden of the old manor house of the neighbouring village. The person who posed the question 'Do you believe in Ghosts?' believed that he was asking a plain question which could be answered with a simple 'yes' or 'no', but actually his question was a highly complicated one, capable of being interpreted in many different ways. The simplest method of interpreting it would be to assume that the questioner meant: 'Do you believe people when they state that they have seen something which they can only assume to be a ghost?' – and the question will be taken in that sense here. If that is all that the inquiry really means, then the answer will undoubtedly be 'yes', for ghosts have been seen by people since the beginning of human history. But if the scope of the question be restricted and held to mean only 'Have *you* personally seen a ghost?' then the answer is likely to be 'no', especially in the case of the male, for comparatively few men claim to have met apparitions. Should the conversation be rendered much more exact and an effort be made to define what precisely is meant by the word 'ghost' then it is likely that all taking part in it will find themselves, at a very early stage of the discussion, in very deep waters.

What is a Ghost?

At one time there was very little doubt about the nature of ghosts, for it was tacitly agreed by everybody that a ghost was a *physical* object, which might be tenuous and hazy in outline, but which was nevertheless material. It was assumed also that the ghost was situated exactly where the observer was seeing it, out there in external space. Some of those taking part in a ghost talk of this kind would probably have added the information that the ghost was a replica of some person who had died recently, or if he had not actually died, was probably, at that very moment, in great distress, his critical condition in all likelihood explaining his appearance there as a ghost. Occasionally, but not very often, an apparition is reported to have been not only visible but audible as well. This was true of the ghost of Hamlet's father, who laid upon the unfortunate Prince of Denmark the grievous burden of avenging his death. But, so far as I know, a ghost has never been so substantial as to have left behind it concrete evidence of its previous presence there, in the way of a neat footprint. Many cases are on record of an apparition having been seen simultaneously by several people but not necessarily by everybody who was present at the time. So also has it often been reported that domestic animals such as dogs, cats and horses have given evidence by their excited behaviour of having seen or heard something unusual and frightening.

The physical theory of an apparition, the theory that it is something material lying out there in space, is nowadays held to be so difficult to maintain that a psychological explanation is preferred by the majority of ghost-experts. And, as will be seen later in this chapter, there are also experts who combine the two theories and who postulate that the apparitions are the result of the intermingling of both physical and psychological factors. But the majority of parapsychologists believe that the whole thing starts with an hallucination on the part of the observer, that is to say with his seeing something, out there in space, which does not actually exist where it appears to be but is the result of an inner activity taking place in the visual centres of his own brain. This does not necessarily mean that the man who claims that he has seen a ghost is a highly imaginative person, or worse still, that he is a person whose mental balance has been temporarily disturbed. This is far from being true of all ghost seers, for many of them have been responsible and completely trustworthy people who have merely testified to the fact that they have witnessed something which, for lack of a better explanation, they have been compelled to call a ghost. And, as has previously been said, their statements have often been corroborated by independent witnesses who were present at that time and who saw, more or less, what they saw.

The Hospital Ghost

I have selected the following example of a ghost out

of the many stories available, and for several reasons. The first reason is that the narrator of the story, Dr. D., has been a friend of mine for many years and I am convinced that in vouching for this story he is not engaged in the gentle art of 'leg-pulling'. The second reason is that Dr. D. is a man of good repute, a consulting physician practising in Harley Street and a member of the staff of a famous London Teaching Hospital which we shall call St. Friar's Hospital. The third is that the 'ghost' in question was encountered in broad daylight and the fourth, that it has also been seen on other occasions by different people. I have to thank Dr. D. for the following description of the St. Friar's Hospital ghost:

'At ten minutes to twelve, on an April day of the year 1938, I was walking down the main corridor of the hospital in the direction of the Medical School. As I was about to enter the open-air part of the corridor, which is flanked on both sides by pillars, I saw a nurse emerge from Number Eight Block and start walking down the corridor towards me. The sun was shining at the time and was casting long shadows of the pillars on to the cement floor of the corridor. I kept my eyes on the approaching figure of the nurse and, although I did not recognize her, I followed the usual hospital custom of taking off my hat to her. Her dress was the regulation hospital dress, blue with small white spots, but somehow it looked to me to be a little "old-fashioned". This was probably because the shoulders were puffed out instead of lying flat and taking the natural curves of her figure. I saw her face sufficiently well to be able to say that she had clear-cut features and that it wore a placid expression. I am also quite sure that, like the pillars, she cast a shadow on to the floor. Had she not suddenly vanished just as she was about to pass me, I should have said that she was, in every way, except for the slight puffing out of the dress over the shoulders, a typical "St. Friar's" Hospital nurse. But she had completely disappeared when only a few yards distant from me!

'I continued on my way to the Medical School, astonished rather than disturbed, delivered my lecture, had my lunch and then, realizing that it was extremely unusual for "St. Friar's" nurses to disappear in this strange way, I decided to talk to the Matron about it. She was not in her office, so I started to tell my story to the Assistant Matron. She stopped me before I had got half-way through it by exclaiming that, without any doubt, I had met the Block Eight ghost! I replied that I had been a great many years at St. Friar's Hospital and had never heard anything about its having a ghost. She explained that a great many nurses had seen it, and that it was now so difficult to get a nurse to go on night duty in Number Eight Block, that the Matron was trying to keep the matter of the ghost as secret as possible. On my inquiring whether there were any story attached to the ghost, she answered that there was. It was said to be the ghost of a nurse who had quarrelled with her ward sister in the eighties of the last century and who, in a fit of pique, had thrown herself over a balcony in Number Eight Block.

'Some years later, during the war, I accidentally learnt that the Hospital Secretary, whilst conducting a journalist round the hospital in order to show him the precautions being taken against fire bombs, had explained to the journalist that it was difficult to get fire-watchers to do duty at night in Block Eight. This was because it was haunted. On being asked by the journalist whether people, other than the nurses, had seen the ghost, the Secretary had replied: "Yes, both Dr. D. and Mr. F., the Clerk of the Works, have met it." On hearing this I went straight to Mr. F. and asked him if it were true that he had seen the Block Eight ghost. He replied that in 1934, between five and six in the evening, he had met it at the open-air part of the corridor. He had noted, as I also had noted, that the nurse looked a little bit "old-fashioned" but for him it was because her skirt was rather long and her cap a trifle unusual. He had indeed called his companion's attention to the oddness in the nurse's uniform and his companion, the then Clerk of the Works, had answered that he had no idea what he was talking about, as there had been no nurse in the corridor. Yet Mr. F., like myself, had watched the nurse approaching for a distance of twenty to thirty yards. Then she had suddenly disappeared! Previously she had been walking towards him with short, quick steps and had appeared to be distressed. But in every other way she appeared to be an ordinary St. Friar's Hospital nurse. Mr. F. told me that he had never seen or heard of any ghost previously and that he had written down and signed a written statement of all that had happened.' So concludes Dr. D.'s account.

A Medium's Account of Ghosts

Most people would regard an encounter with a ghost

as an astonishing event, but to a medium it is all in the day's work and scarcely worth putting on record. In her book *This World and That* Miss Phoebe Payne tells us how when motoring with her secretary back from Scotland they were compelled to pass the night in an old inn, which had formerly been a well-known posting inn. Whilst obtaining something to eat before going to bed she realized that the old house was haunted and that the inner of the two rooms that they had chosen 'had a much stronger atmosphere of haunt' than the bedroom to be occupied by her secretary. Miss Payne continues her story thus: 'I fell asleep immediately but only to be awakened some hours later by a sense of suffocation, feeling two hands round my neck. Opening my eyes, I saw bending over me a pale-faced man, with a mask over his eyes. He was dressed in a dark green travelling coat and three-cornered hat, and looked in every way like the story-book highwayman. By that time I was choking and was furiously angry at what I felt to be an unwarrantable attack, so I sat up in bed and told him, in no measured terms, what I thought. In the usual way of ghosts when challenged in a positive spirit, he disappeared into thin air, leaving me with a bruised neck – or at least, it felt bruised though there were no marks to be seen.

'At breakfast next morning I said to the maid, "I don't like your ghost, he might be dangerous to some people." She stammered an excuse and went on to say it was just imagination. I said calmly, "Don't be silly, you know perfectly well this place is haunted by a highwayman," and she then admitted that once in a while this happened, and it often frightened people who slept in that particular room.'[1]

Fortunately Miss Payne was aware of the fact that fear makes ghosts 'of an unpleasant and malicious type dangerous and the right treatment of ghosts of this kind is to have no fear'. She is of the opinion that just as 'the weak waves reaching a radio receiver are amplified by means of the electrical energy in the set, so does fear amplify the psychic impact from within the psycho-physical organisms of the victim. The point is that without both the fear and the belief that physical damage would result the repercussion would not take place. It is not the ghost who kills the victim but the victim who kills himself through fear.'

Miss Phoebe Payne ends her chapter on the subjects of ghosts and haunts by telling us how to deal with any ghosts which are annoying to us. She warns us not to lose one's temper with them for 'this may cause an explosion which drives the ghost out of existence for good. The great thing, in short, is to treat the majority of ghosts rather casually and not to take them too seriously, nor even to be too much interested in them . . . otherwise one may actually give them the energy which they need to recharge themselves and keep the pattern going.'

Miss Payne's advice concerning the handling of ghosts sounds excellent but it may be a little bit difficult to put into practice. I must confess that, never having met an apparition previously I should be inclined to take far more interest in its appearance and its

[1] *This World and That*, by P. D. Payne and L. Bendit.

behaviour than she considers to be appropriate. Whilst I am confident that I should not lose my temper with a ghost 'and drive it out of existence for good', I think that I should find it difficult to treat it in precisely the right off-hand manner.

That ghosts are not great rarities, even in countries inhabited by so unimaginative and sober-minded a people as the English, was revealed by the special Census of Apparitions which was taken by the S.P.R. soon after it had started its investigation of paranormal phenomena in the year 1882. A form was sent out to 17,000 people in which a request was made for an answer to the following question: 'Have you ever, when believing yourself to be completely awake, had a vivid impression of seeing or being touched by a living being or inanimate object, or hearing a voice; which impression, so far as you could discover, was not due to any external cause?' Replies were received from 15,316 people out of the 17,000 circulated, and 9.9 per cent of those who replied answered 'Yes'. It was noted also that the great majority of those who claimed to have experienced an apparition were women. People who had returned a 'yes' to the question were written to again and were asked to give additional information, such as whether the appearance of the apparition had synchronized with some tragic event elsewhere, for example the death of a relative or friend. This question was asked in order to find out whether telepathy was likely to be a factor in the production of the apparition in question, the idea being that in critical situations telepathic messages are more likely to be sent out than when nothing unusual is happening.

An analysis of the replies showed that only thirty coincidences of the apparition with the death of a relative or friend had occurred in the 1,900 replies received, an incidence of only one in forty-three. Although the coincidences with death were few, and not always exact coincidences, there seemed to be a tendency for the appearance of apparitions to be clustered around the time of a relative's or friend's demise and this meant that the action of telepathy could not be entirely excluded. Statistics were also obtained of the incidence of what are usually called Collective Apparitions, that is to say apparitions seen or heard simultaneously by several people. Collective Apparitions constituted nine per cent of all the apparitions reported.

One of the best works on the subject of apparitions is the book written by the late G. N. M. Tyrell and published in 1951, and I take this opportunity of acknowledging my indebtedness to it. Tyrell starts by dividing apparitions into four different classes: (i) *Experimental cases*, or those cases in which the *agent* or person mainly responsible for the appearance of the apparition has deliberately projected himself, by a deliberate effort of will, into another person's presence; (ii) *Crises apparitions*, or those seen or heard about the time of some crisis such as death; (iii) *Apparitions* which have appeared so long after such a crisis that the latter cannot be held responsible for them; (iv) *Apparitions* which have long been known to haunt certain areas or premises. These four classes of ghosts are not sharply defined but tend to shade off into one another. But in spite of this they provide a useful basis for descriptive purposes.

A good instance of the deliberately projected type of apparition was given in Chapter 3 (page 67) and the following example has been taken from Dr. and Mrs. Bendit's book *This World and That*. Dr. Bendit tells us that for a long time he had been pondering over a psychological problem and that he suddenly remembered a friend of his who might be able to help him to solve it. The person in question was a military man who had left England and was now living in a country in South Eastern Europe. Dr. Bendit continues his story as follows: 'Though I sat in my own room in England, alert and in full waking consciousness, it seemed as though a part of my mind travelled out through space. In a few seconds I felt as though I were in two places at once. The stationary "me" was aware of the room I was in, the rough texture of the chair-cover under my fingers, and all the usual things surrounding me; but the travelled part of my mind seemed to shoot through space, rather like an arrow winging its way to a target. In what seemed like a flash of time this moving part of me found itself in a place it had never seen. It was a bare office. I carefully noted the position of the door, the window, filing cabinets and large office table. Seated at a desk, writing, was my friend, dressed in uniform.

'The strange thing that struck me at the time was that, although he continued to write, some part of his mind appeared to know that I was there, and at once a telepathic *rapport* was set up which, in some odd fashion, enabled me mentally to discuss my problem with him. His mind grasped what was needed, and quickly gave me the answer I wanted. As soon as this happened the telepathic line of communication was switched off, and I had a queer feeling of my mind returning along the track by which it had gone out.

'Not knowing what to make of this vivid experience I immediately drew a plan of the office in which I had been, marking the correct pieces of furniture, door and window. This I posted to a woman who lived in the same city as my military friend. She knew us both so I wrote explaining what had happened but I did not tell her the nature of the problem which had been unravelled.

'About six months later she came to England, and when we met she said, "Your plan of Jan's room was absolutely correct. He told me to tell you that he had not only been mentally aware of your presence, but was quite clear about the difficulty you were in." She then told me the problem itself, so that we were able to check the correctness of what Jan had reported.

'There has always existed a strong mental affinity between myself and this particular friend, but it was the only time it operated in this way and at a long distance.'

Many good examples of the second category of Crises Apparitions are available and the example quoted below has been taken from the album of apparitions collected by Edmund Gurney and published under the title, *Phantasms of the Living*. The story is told in the first person by the percipient, a woman whose brother, an airman, had been shot down in France on 19 March 1917, early in the morning. She herself was in India at that time. 'My brother,' she says, 'appeared to me on the same day 19 March 1917. At the time I was either sewing or talking to my baby – I cannot remember quite what I was doing at the moment. The baby was on the bed. I had a very strong feeling that I must turn round; on doing so I saw my brother, Aldred A. Bowyer-Bower. Thinking he was alive and had been sent out to India, I was simply delighted to see him, and turned round quickly to put the baby in a safe place on the bed, so that I could go on talking to my brother; then I turned again and put my hand out to him and I found that he was not there. I thought he was only joking, so I called him and looked everywhere I could think of looking. It was only when I could not find him that I became very frightened and the awful fear came to me that he might be dead. I felt very sick and giddy. I think it was two o'clock when the baby was christened and in the church I felt he was there again, but I could not see him. Two weeks later I saw in the paper that he was missing. Yet I could not bring myself to believe that he had passed away.'[1]

Tyrell's fourth type of apparition is a very familiar one. It is the conservative unenterprising kind of ghost which haunts a certain limited area and which is always to be seen doing the same thing. It is the 'Grey Lady' who glides down a certain garden path and who invariably disappears when she reaches a certain spot. Or it appears as the monk who haunts the ruined cloisters of a monastery or it may manifest itself merely as the sound of footsteps heard in the corridor of the West wing of some old Scottish castle. There is no need to describe apparitions of this dull, unimaginative, haunting type, for they conform to a standard pattern

[1] Quoted by G. N. M. Tyrell in *Apparitions*.

of appearance and of behaviour and never do anything surprising. But, as Tyrell has pointed out, there is a certain quality in these haunting spectres and in their behaviour, which is a little bit puzzling to us. They resemble certain dead individuals sufficiently well for everybody to recognize whom they represent but when they and their actions are looked into more carefully there is something odd or missing in them. There is an emptiness and a somnolence in their behaviour which renders it entirely different to that of the people whom they are supposed to represent. After noting it we are no longer surprised that the ancient Greeks called hesitant and uncertain people of this kind 'the Shades'. Nor is it surprising that the Greeks believed that in the process of losing their bodies and becoming Shades, the dead had lost all their former hold on life, so that all that they were capable of doing was to wander aimlessly and forever down the dreary passages of Pluto's gloomy underworld. So also is it likely that Homer was referring to this emptiness of the 'Shades' when he wrote that there was 'no heart in them'.

Carrington on Haunted Places

Whateley Carrington has propounded an interesting theory about haunted places and the ability of certain people to recognize that they are haunted. He postulates that the mind is made up of a number of different units which he called *psychons*. He pictures these 'psychons' as having many similarities with those well-known psychological entities, the 'complexes', and he suggests that when a person has become very strongly identified with a certain place, such as a house or a garden, the psychon related to it may become detached from his mind and may anchor itself to the place in question. According to Carrington's theory detached psychons carry with them a certain load of 'psychic energy', so that when the person dies and a 'medium' or 'sensitive' visits the haunted spot he or she becomes aware of the fact that the house or garden is highly charged with feeling. Whether Carrington's theory is of any value or not, there is very little doubt that sensitive people often react very strongly to places which they have never visited before and declare them to be either tragic or happy in accordance with their own emotional response to them. According to Carrington psychons are midway between matter and mind and they are capable of surviving, as independent units, only for a limited length of time.

Myers's Theory of Apparitions

Myers was the first person, so far as I know, to put forward a theory to the effect that the apparitions of both the living and the dead are phenomena of a telepathic nature. Reduced to its simplest form Myers's theory proclaims that whilst struggling with some emotional crisis, the *agent* or person responsible for the apparition sends forth a telepathic cry of distress which the distant recipient receives and then embodies in some sensory form, thus converting what was previously too vague to be described, into a full-blown apparition. This theory was advanced by Myers in the year 1888 and it has now been accepted by a great many modern psychical research workers. Like all other theories about apparitions, Myers's theory has its weaknesses and one of these is that it fails to explain satisfactorily Collective Apparitions, or the simultaneous perception of an apparition by two, three or more people. It is possible of course to assume that when sending out his telepathic cry of distress, the *agent* dispatched it simultaneously to several of his friends and that they all received his message and gave it substance. But this is unsatisfactory for in Collective cases the apparition has sometimes been seen or heard by a bystander who was entirely unknown to the agent, and examples could be given in which the unknown bystander was the only person to see the apparition.

Gurney realized this weakness in Myers's theory of apparition and he did his best to remedy it. He saw three ways of overcoming the difficulties occasioned by Collective Apparitions, the first being to postulate that the phantom was not entirely an hallucination but that something was actually present, as a material essence, out there where it was seen. But Gurney held that the *agent* was partly responsible for the appearance of the apparition out there, for he influenced the various recipients telepathetically, so that they clothed what was only a material essence with the imagery necessary to render it recognizable. Gurney's second method of explaining apparitions was to suppose that the *agent's* telepathic influences were entirely concentrated on the single percipient B, with whom he had had strong personal links and that B transmitted what he had seen by the same telepathic means to C, who in turn passed the image on to the percipient F. Gurney likened this spreading process of images to the process by which infection can be spread amongst people.

The chief objection to Gurney's rather complicated theory is that it does not really explain why telepathetically-projected images should be shared by two or more people merely because they happen to be near together in space. The said people not only discover the apparition simultaneously but they receive telepathetically precisely the same image and find nothing incongruous in it, even though they are all looking at the image from different viewpoints. How can all this be done telepathetically? This fact that the visual images of a Collective apparition seem to be entirely appropriate to the particular angle from which the apparition is being viewed by each person makes Gurney's modification of Myers's theory a difficult one to accept. Tyrell illustrates this flaw in the Gurney theory by quoting accounts of apparitions taken from Gurney's own book, *Phantasms of the Living*. He cites the case of a percipient who first caught sight of an apparition whilst he was lying in his bed; who saw it next from a window; then, having walked right through the apparition he views it yet a third time whilst standing at the door. 'If it be granted,' Tyrell writes, 'as I think it reasonably must be, that the perception of apparitions is a full-blown perception, identical in its features with normal perception and that, as the figures move, the sensory images of all the percipients change, exactly as they would if the figure were a natural one, then Gurney's theory of collective perception breaks down. For it might be conceived that one percipient should telepathetically affect another so as to cause him to see a figure *more or less* like the one he was seeing himself, but it is inconceivable that the figures should be *exactly* correlated to one another as a normal perception. Indeed, experimental telepathy suggests that the figures seen by different participants would be likely to differ a good deal from one another.'

Tyrell's Theory of Apparitions

Tyrell's own explanation of apparitions is highly ingenious but it is also a little bit complicated, as perhaps a solution of so difficult a problem as this is bound to be. He first discusses the nature of the messages which are telepathetically communicated by the *agent* to the *percipient* or *percipients* and he comes to the conclusion that the original message can only be the transmission of a vague idea which he calls the *theme* or general *motif*. He suggests that this *theme* is very loosely formulated by the agent but that it possesses great emotional intensity. Before an apparition can appear the theme has to be given substance and Tyrell likens this further development of the theme to the process of producing a play. He speaks of the *apparitional drama* and he calls into being such imaginary theatrical personages as the Producer and the Stage Carpenter. These figures are of course personifications of certain little understood faculties in the subconscious regions of the minds of the agent and the percipient, creative faculties which Tyrell calls 'the mid-level constituents of man's personality'. According to him these constituents are entities which are intermediate in nature between mind and matter and it is their job to produce what he calls an *idea pattern*. They manage to do this in an automatic and unconscious manner, in the poorly-lit mid-level regions of the two minds concerned with the apparition production. It is part of Tyrell's thesis that these mid-level constituents of one individual's mind are not entirely cut off from similar mid-level constituents in other individual minds, as are the higher levels of these minds. They communicate very readily with one another and this allows of the producer and the stage carpenter of one mind collaborating with the greatest ease with the stage carpenter and the producer of another mind. As Professor H. H. Price has put it in his preface to Tyrell's book: 'According to Tyrell the word "telepathy" is just a way of referring to the *non-separate* character which mid-levels of different personalities have. In these mid-level strata, the notion of spatial apartness no longer applies. So if I see an apparition of you the plot of this apparitional drama is the result of the joint efforts of your "producer" and mine.'

Tyrell's view that the mid-levels of the mind which make direct contact with the corresponding levels of other minds, is no new idea, for it appears in a somewhat different form in Jung's theory of the Collective Unconscious. Tyrell's idea may seem strange at first but it has this advantage that it explains not only the difficult phenomenon of telepathy but also the problem of the Collective Apparition. The existence of a common mind around us of which we all partake is an idea also to be found in the philosophy of that twelfth century Moslem mystic, Averroes. This subject will be discussed at greater length in the final chapter of this book.

10

The Survival Problem

Belief in some sort of survival of death is almost universal and even palaeolithic man buried his dead with flint axe-heads and supplies of food in the hope that these would prove helpful to them in the after-life. There are very few countries in which the hope of eventual reunion with those who have passed on previously has not helped to mitigate the sorrows of bereavement. So widespread is this belief in some sort of life after death that it might almost be said to be instinctive in mankind. But are widely spread and instinctive hopes more likely to be fulfilled than less prevalent ones? Some would say 'yes'. Ruysbroek would certainly have returned such an answer, for he wrote that 'As hunger presupposes bread, so does man's longing after God presuppose God'. And the hope for, and belief in, some sort of existence after death is as strong and as widely spread as is belief in the existence of a Deity. It is not to be dismissed peremptorily as a produce of man's imagination.

When we investigate further and look at the various forms of survival which have been pictured by those who have hoped for it we find that all unanimity disappears and that we are examining a medley of beliefs, many of them incompatible with one another. Many people have pictured a form of life beyond the grave which differs very little, if at all, from the life they have lived on earth and even the philosophers have at times subscribed to such a view of an after-life. But as a rule people look forward to an improvement in their lot after death. For example, the ancient Egyptians looked forward to existence in a far more fertile country than their native Egypt, a land in which astonishingly fine harvests were reaped without difficulty or fatigue. The old Teutonic races saw themselves drinking their favourite mead out of great goblets in the vast halls of Valhalla, whilst American Indians dreamed of happy hunting grounds of a quality they had never seen before on earth.

The term 'future life' is as ambiguous as is the term 'survival'. It can mean either the durational existence of some immortal element in man or else it can mean immortality in the sense of a *timeless* existence. In his writings Plato gives an account of both of these entirely different conceptions of life after death. 'There is the doctrine of the *Symposium* which is not of a future life but of a timeless existence, attainable here and now, by an escape from the flux of time. There is the other doctrine of the *Phaedo*, involving pre-existence and post-existence which are concepts possessing meaning only with regard to the temporal life of the soul.'[1]

We have to admit that whenever the term 'immortal soul' is used we are immediately landed in difficulties, for there exists no agreement amongst the priests and the philosophers as to what the immortal soul in man actually is. Plato tells us that the 'soul is substance and that substance is indestructible'. Yet according to the

[1] S. Rhadakrishnan, *The Brahma Sutra*.

Neo-Platonists and, it would seem, also according to Christ, a soul can be destroyed if it rebels against the higher principles. The Eastern philosophers and religious teachers are much more explicit on this difficult subject than are Western philosophers and priests. According to the Advaita Vedanta, two entities in man have to be considered when the question of the soul and its survival is being discussed. There is the individual 'self' or *jiva* which undoubtedly undergoes a crisis at death and there is also in man that Divine element the *Atman*, which is the immutable Consciousness or greater Self which man shares with all his fellow men. The *Atman* survives after the complex of elements which constitutes a man's *personal* existence has ceased to be of any interest or importance to him. It may be said therefore that according to the Vedantist all that is *personal* in a man perishes at his death and only that greater and much more comprehensive Self, the *Atman*, survives.

But this statement needs qualification. Hindus believe in the doctrine of re-incarnation, a doctrine which has also made a strong appeal to many Western philosophers. Schopenhauer subscribed to it and David Hume remarked that it was 'the only system of this kind that philosophy can hearken to'. The Christian and the Vedantist both look upon this life on earth as being a school for the instruction of souls, but the Vedantist feels that many re-incarnations will be required before the soul is fit to be transferred to the Celestial regions. Swedenborg also found it difficult to accept the Protestant's view that after death, the soul was immediately transported to Heaven or to the Infernal regions. He fell back on the idea that the dead passed through an intermediate state mid-way between the heights of Heaven and the depths of Hell. Heaven requires the conjunction in man of the good and the true and Hell the conjunction in him of evil and falsity, and the inhabitants of Swedenborg's intermediate realm were neither completely the one nor the other. This being so they were unfitted for life in Heaven until the false and the evil in them had been eliminated. Swedenborg went so far as to declare that when a man first entered this intermediate world his face and his tone of voice were similar to what they were when he was alive on earth, but that afterwards they underwent a change. In the later stage of his development man's *outer appearance* corresponded with his *inner state* for, according to Swedenborg 'no one is allowed to counterfeit affections which were not properly his own'.

The Intermediate State

The Catholics are also more logical than are the Protestants in that they realize the necessity for postulating the existence of an intermediate stage in man's spiritual development. Instead of being promoted immediately and automatically to life in Heaven as a consequence of the mere act of dying, the Catholic Church envisages the soul of the ordinary man as passing, for a time, into the probationary stage of Purgatory. There it remains until it has attained the qualities which are necessary to life in the Celestial Regions. According to the Catholic Church only the saint is in a spiritual condition which permits of his passing directly to Heaven.

Buddhism

The Tibetan Buddhists also believe in the existence of an intermediate state into which the spirit passes immediately after the death of the body, a state known to them as the *Bardo*. They place great emphasis on the need for maintaining consciousness as long as possible in the process of dying so that the dying person may have time to realize what is happening to him. Otherwise his spirit is likely to be liberated in a confused state, so troubled and alarmed at the change which has occurred in its form of existence, that it is unable to tolerate the Clear Light of the Void and struggles to return and to reoccupy the comforting darkness of selfhood and the place which it formerly had on the earth. From the intermediate state of the *Bardo* the spirit may pass, after a variable period of time into another body, to be reborn into the world. Or in some cases, the spirit has reached full enlightenment and with it freedom from the *Samsara* or the round of earthly existences. In other words the individual in question has attained *Nirvana*.

What is there in man which is capable of surviving the death of his body?

If any demonstration were needed of the superficial way in which we think about the mystery of death it was provided by a series of articles on survival which was published by the *Sunday Times* in 1959. These articles were contributed by a number of intelligent and highly educated people, yet only one of them – and he a Hindu – stopped to consider two essential questions: first. the meaning of the word 'survival', and second, whether or not there exists anything in man which is capable of withstanding the disintegration of his body. The others plunged straightaway into a description of the nature of the after-life, a description which, quite naturally, was pre-determined by the background of his philosophical and religious thought.

It is inevitable that the answer we return to the great riddle of death should be a subjective one, and all that the writer of this book is able to do is to give his own individual answer to it. But two preliminary questions have to be answered. The first is: 'What is there in man which has the capacity to survive the cataclysm of death? and the second is: 'What is the nature of the true Self?' In other words: 'Who am I?' Few Europeans ask themselves this fundamental question, yet in India it is one of the first to be put to a *chela* by his *guru*. And when the answer eventually comes to the *chela* it comes, not by way of clever reasoning, but it is revealed to him as the results of his own insight. The process is always the same in this finding of the true Self. One by one the layers of the not-self are stripped off until that single Reality described by the Hindus as *Sachidananda*, a state of being in which Consciousness, Being and Bliss are blended, is approached. Obviously my body is not my 'self', for it is continually changing; it possesses no permanence and it will crumble into dust at my death. Nor has that jumble of mental, moving and emotional features by which my acquaintances recognize me, any right to call itself my 'self'. Like my body it possesses no permanence and it is far too dependent on my body to survive such an upheaval as the body's death. Nor do I think so highly of this kaleidoscope of changing qualities which is called my personality to deem it worthy of being granted the doubtful boon of an endless persistence in time. My personality is an obstacle and not an aid to the discovery of my real Self and it is only when it has been silenced and for the time being rendered passive that I am able to find what I have been searching for. Then, at last, may I catch sight of a greater Self which embraces so much more than my ordinary self does that I am unable to define its limits. All that I can say about this state of being is that when I approach it I get some understanding of what the Hindu is trying to convey to me when he utters the well-known words: 'The Knower, that which is Known and the act of Knowing become one.' If anything within me is capable of surviving the cataclysm of death, it is surely this greater Self.

We take difficult questions far too simply and there are many questions which cannot be answered with a plain 'Yes' or 'No'. This is true even of many scientific questions. For example, physicists started by regarding an electron as being a *particle* and then at a later date they started to describe it as a *wave*. *Now* when we inquire of them whether an electron is a particle or a wave, they reply that in some cases it behaves as a particle and in other cases as a wave. This being so, an electron 'is neither a particle or a wave. It is *both*.' So also is it impossible to return a plain 'Yes' or a plain 'No' to this complicated question 'Does man survive the death of his body or not?' The answer I have returned to it will be regarded by many people as just the sort of answer a mystic would give, and mystics, being muddled-headed dreamers, it will not be acceptable to many readers. This being so, it is only right that I should supplement my own views by expressing those of other people. I have selected for this purpose the views of two well-known philosophers, Professor C. D. Broad and Professor H. H. Price.

Professor Broad's Views on Survival

Professor C. D. Broad dealt with the problem of survival in an address which he gave to the S.P.R. in 1958. He started by stating that the great majority of those who believed in a personal form of survival insisted on the need for the persistence of some sort of *physical* structure capable of supporting the elaborate system of 'dispositions, cognitive, conative and emotional, which constitute human nature, and also the personal characteristics of that particular individual'. He then advanced the usual Cartesian dualistic view of man that he was an intimate association of two different constituents, the first being his body and the second something which carried with it the 'organized dispositional basis of man's personality'. To this second constituent of man he applied the terms *Psi-component*. Unlike many dualists Broad assures us that there is no need to assume that this second constituent of man is devoid of all the qualities possessed by a 'physical existent'. There are, he says, physical existents 'which are extended and in a sense localized, which have persistent structure and are the seat of rhythmic modulations, which are not in any sense ordinary bodies but which are closely associated with a body of a certain kind'. He gives as an example of a structure which possesses all these properties 'an electromagnetic field associated with a conductor carrying an electric current'. A second example of a physical existent with these qualities is the transmitting beam coming from a wireless station. Professor Broad continues thus: 'And perhaps to think that *nothing* carrying the dispositional basis of a man's personality *could* exist after the death of the body is as if one should imagine that nothing corresponding to the performance of an orchestral piece at a wireless transmitting station could exist anywhere in space after the station which broadcast it had been destroyed.'

Professor Price's View of Survival

Professor H. H. Price of New College, Oxford, has also addressed the S.P.R. on the question of personal survival and he has given us a detailed picture of an after-life constructed out of 'mental images'. Hamlet withdrew from the act of self-destruction because he felt that bad dreams might disturb his peace of mind after he had 'shuffled off this mortal coil', and if Professor Price be right his fears were fully justified. He pictures the dead as producing for themselves images of seemingly solid bodies, bodies which will seem as real to them as the bodies they have lost. But existence in this world of mental images will be confusing. The Professor writes that 'a wish to go to Oxford might be immediately followed by the occurrence of a vivid and detailed set-up of Oxford-like images'.

I have no liking for this dream variety of personal survival which Professor Price has offered me and I can find only one advantage in it, the single advantage that existence in a world of mental images frees us from any necessity to state where in space, this after-world is situated. Dreams and mental images are situated in a private space of their own, or perhaps it would be more accurate to say that being devoid of all spatial properties they require no accommodation anywhere. This means that in order to pass from the tangible world of the living into the dream world of the dead no movement in space will be necessary. We should think of the passage as a change of consciousness, very similar to that which occurs when we change from wakefulness to sleep.

Professor Price places great emphasis on an idea which has been frequently mentioned in this book, the idea that human minds are less isolated from one another then we believe them to be. As a result of their freedom they may overlap and even coalesce with one another in their unconscious depths so as to form what has been called 'group-minds'. This overlapping makes it easier for the dead to keep in touch with one another in the after-worlds sketched by the two professors, but even with this advantage a doubt still enters my mind. Will those people who insist on some personal form of survival be content with the after-world with which the two professors have provided them? I very much doubt this, for as I see it, the after-worlds of Professors Broad and Price resemble very closely the Plutonic realms of the Ancient Greeks, an after-world for which I personally have a strong distaste.

When the Buddha was asked by his disciples whether or not man survived the death of his body, he is said 'to have maintained a noble silence'. He did this because he discouraged theoretical questions amongst his followers. His mission was to teach them how to escape from suffering and not to instruct them in metaphysics. But when, a little later, his disciple, Ananda, reopened with him the question of man's survival of death, he replied, quite simply, that in one sense man survived death and that in another sense he did not. Perhaps this is all that can be usefully said on this very obscure subject.

Christianity and the Idea of Eternal Life

There exists and has long existed a great deal of confusion in Christian thought on the subject of Eternal Life, a confusion which is in great part due to a mistranslation of the Greek word *aiōn* or *aeon*. This word was used in connexion with a philosophical idea which is no longer fashionable, the idea that there exist two different worlds, side by side, the visible world of 'time' and 'becoming' and the invisible and timeless world of 'being'. The word *aiōn*, which means eternal, was a characteristic of the second of these two worlds, the changeless and invisible world of being. The world of being was held to be of an entirely different quality to the familiar world of becoming. Here, in this world of becoming, in which we now live, everything is in a ceaseless state of flux. Here all things change, some more slowly in terms of geological ages and others, like our bodies, much more quickly, so that we rapidly become old. Outside ourselves we observe this ceaseless stream of becoming and within us we catch sight of a corresponding flux of changing thoughts and feelings.

Behind and beyond this ever-changing and visible

world of time, the philosophers have postulated the existence of an unchanging *world* of *being*, a world which lies neither in Space nor Time. This was the Eternal World which was believed to contain within itself not only all things but all possibilities also. Spinoza had in mind a world of this kind when he wrote that Eternity could 'not be defined by Time or have any relation to it'. Plato was also referring to it when he stated that the order and the relationships of the '*aeonian* world' were timeless and that the things and the events which we saw in this present changing world of time were but weak and imperfect reflections of the things and events to be found in the Eternal World of 'being'.

These old philosophical ideas are no longer fashionable and instead of looking upon Eternal Life as a different state of 'being', Christians are now inclined to regard Eternal Life as a life which goes on for ever and ever. Living as we do in a culture which regards quantity as of greater importance than quality we are rapidly substituting the idea of *quantity* of life for that of *quality* of life. But this is contrary to early Christian teaching, for as Maurice Nicoll has said: 'To lay hold of *eternal* life refers to some possibility in *this* life, to some change that a man can undergo here – or at least begin to put himself in the way of. From this deeper standpoint no true psychology of man can exist without this goal being recognized as the aim . . . The end of man is the attainment of this further state of himself. His real explanation lies in this fact.'[1]

---

[1] Maurice Nicoll, *Living Time and the Integration of Life*.

The Medium's Evidence in Favour of a Personal Survival

The fact that the spiritualist accepts evidence which favours the idea of a personal survival of death uncritically and that the great majority of mediums have at one time or another, been guilty of fraud, does not justify our dismissing as of no account all evidence coming from spiritualistic sources. The temptations to which mediums are subjected are exceedingly great. Good mediums are rare and this means that the supply of them does not meet demands. It also implies that so long as a medium is able to satisfy the requirements of his patrons he will make a good living but that when he proves disappointing to his clients he is likely to be replaced by somebody else. Now the phenomena of the séance – and more particularly physical phenomena, such as materializations – are extraordinarily fickle and erratic, sometimes taking place and sometimes failing to appear. In the latter case, the medium, semi-conscious though he may be, senses the general feeling of dissatisfaction and in order to produce what is expected of him he may resort to fraud. The credulity of those who attend séances and their lack of discrimination makes progress along the path of crookedness astonishingly easy for a medium and many years may pass before he is found out. This does not necessarily mean that all the phenomena he helps to produce are fraudulent. It means only that some are due to trickery whilst others may be genuine, and this makes it very difficult to estimate the worth of the medium's evidence for personal survival. Hence the need for great caution in accepting spiritualistic testimony in favour of it.

How does the Medium Work?

The second question which requires answering is how the medium works and I wish here to acknowledge my indebtedness to Dr. and Mrs. Bendit and to their book *This World and That*[1] for information on this subject. Mrs. Bendit, better known to many people by her maiden name, Miss Phoebe Payne, defines a medium as a person 'who has the ability to dissociate his or her personality in a particular way, and at a particular level'. Dissociation brings with it a lowering of the level of consciousness which varies in different mediums from a condition of slight drowsiness up to a state of deep trance. Miss Payne describes the medium's condition as being 'a half-way state . . . a condition of slight self-hypnosis, wherein the mediumistic person loses clearcut perception of his environment, which seems to recede to the far end of a tunnel'. The majority of mediums fall into a semi-trance state and this means that although they seem to be oblivious of what is happening around them, they are much more aware of everything than onlookers imagine them to be.

The Spiritual Guide or Control

Most mediums state that they do not come into

[1] Phoebe Payne and Lawrence Bendit, *This World and That*.

direct contact with the dead but that they reach them indirectly through the agency of a 'control' or 'spiritual guide'. The usual procedure at a séance is first that the medium goes into the dissociated or semi-trance state, in which his or her personality appears to withdraw and to be replaced by the personality of the 'spiritual guide'. Sometimes the 'spiritual guide' who now takes charge of the medium announces his name to the audience, and sometimes he indulges in a short preliminary talk on such general subjects as philosophy and ethics. It is noteworthy that the 'guides' who appear at spiritualistic séances are almost always romantic, picturesque and extremely interesting people, such as an old Indian chief, a priest from ancient Egypt, or an inhabitant of the lost continent of Atlantis. It is not in the least surprising that spiritual guides should be invested with so much glamour and romance, for they are almost always people for whom the medium has, and always has had, a very high regard. In all probability they are dramatizations of the mediums' own personalities and more particularly of those features in their characters which have never been given a chance to manifest themselves in the humdrum circumstances of the mediums' lives. Now, at long last, in the limelight of the spiritualistic séance, these sub-personalities have been given the opportunity to assert themselves. But as Mrs. Bendit has pointed out, a 'spiritual guide' is a symbol of the medium's most cherished ideals and, as such, it is invested with positive value for that particular person. It would be a mistake, therefore, for anyone else to make light of what the medium rates so highly.

Whateley Carrington's Investigation of Spiritual Guides

Carrington designed a series of experiments in the hope of unravelling the relationship existing between the medium, his 'spiritual controls' and his discarnate communicators. He chose for investigation that very well-known and very successful medium, Mrs. Leonard, a woman who, during her long career as a medium, was never known to resort to any form of trickery. Carrington made use of 'word association' tests in order to distinguish between the various entities in a medium. Psychologists often employ association tests as an aid to psycho-analysis and Carrington applied them to Mrs. Leonard, first in her ordinary state and then in the state when a 'spirit guide' was said to be in control of her. He found that the time she took to react to the list of words and to what she associated with them differed in these two different psychological states. Mrs. Leonard claimed that her usual control was a young woman, by name Feda, and because Feda was only a secondary personality of Mrs. Leonard's, it seemed likely that Feda would display substantially the same time-reactions as Mrs. Leonard had shown. This was what Carrington expected, but it was far from being what actually happened. On applying the tests . . . 'Feda showed a most remarkable tendency to give short reaction times where Mrs. Leonard gave long, and long where Mrs. Leonard gave short. In fact, she appeared to be, in some important sense, the *mirror-image* or *opposite*, of the normal personality, and the tendency was strong enough to indicate a true connexion between the two just as unmistakably as if a *positive* resemblance had been found.'

As a result of his experiments, Carrington reached the following conclusion on the subject of 'spirit guides', a conclusion which will be given in his own words: 'I drew the conclusion, which I have no reason to doubt, that Feda is to be regarded as a secondary personality of Mrs. Leonard, formed probably round a nucleus of repressed material. But although I believe this to be true, it does not necessarily settle the onto-logical status of Feda quite so finally as might be supposed. I say that she is a secondary personality of Mrs. Leonard; but I am not sure that she is *only* a secondary personality. For, fantastic as it may sound, I am not at all sure that epistemologically speaking, a personality formed by budding, or splitting, or dis-sociation, or whatever you like to call it, may not have just as good a claim to be considered a *real* personality, in its own right, as one formed in the usual way – whatever that may be.'

By this Carrington implies that if personal survival be true, then after Mrs. Leonard's physical death, Feda – a selection made by Mrs. Leonard's imagination – has as good a chance of surviving as has the personality from which the selection of Feda was contrived. He drew another important conclusion from these experi-ments on Mrs. Leonard. Whenever a medium has given information concerning some dead person it is always difficult to decide whether this information has been imparted by a discarnate spirit, or whether it has been derived telepathetically from a living person. As a result of his experiments with Mrs. Leonard, Carring-ton came to the conclusion that the two alternatives were not so mutually exclusive as he had previously thought them to be. They will remain mutually exclusive only for 'so long as we think of telepathy in the same kind of way that we think of telephones, and of what we call "mind-reading", in terms of books of reference. If we think of the medium as looking up a fact in the mind of a sitter almost as she might do in a dictionary, then *ex-hypothesi* no communicator has anything to do with it. But my whole doubt rests on the fact that it is *ex-hypothesi* whereas, if we were to think of what is going on in other – and to me more plausible – terms, we might find that the question falls to the ground.'[1] What Carrington believes to be 'going on' in cases of telepathy is that, because in their unconscious depths *all* minds are liable to overlap and even to coalesce, ideas cannot be said to be more in one mind than in another mind. Consequently it is a waste of time to discuss whether an idea passed from mind X to mind Y, for it can be said to belong to X-Y mind, a mind which blends in its depths with countless other minds. More recently, Dr. Gardner Murphy has developed this same idea of an *interpersonal* mental field possessing properties which cannot be expressed in terms of any one individual mind. So also is it implicit in the ancient teaching of Raja Yoga and in the philosophy of Averroes.

The Medium's Testimony

In arriving at a decision on the subject of personal survival the evidence supplied by mediums must be taken into account, but unfortunately the majority of

[1] Whateley Carrington, *The Meaning of Survival*.

mediums are not very reliable witnesses. Miss Phoebe Payne, herself a medium, fully realizes how few of the people attending spiritualistic séances are capable of estimating the value of the evidence obtained there in favour of a personal form of survival. Their minds are already committed to accepting everything they see and hear at its face value, and they are disposed to regard with strong disfavour anybody who examines it at all critically. She formulates admirably what a person's attitude to this evidence should be. All that he is in a position to say is: 'This is true to me at the present moment. I know also that as I learn more this truth will change. My mind is a finite, limited thing and it can only show me one aspect of reality at a time. But what I have learned is that there is a reality which is inalienable, indestructible and inexpressible . . . Logic and reason can lead me towards that reality. They can also lead me away from it, by preventing me from considering imponderables. They are thus dangerous guides if I allow them to master me, but they are useful servants if I, the spiritual learner and knower, use them and direct them.'

The minds of the people who attend spiritualistic séances exert a strong influence on what happens there and their unconscious memories are much more likely to be tapped by the medium than are their more conscious memories. Miss Phoebe Payne writes: 'Another characteristic of the unconscious is that it is a field where desire, and not objective thinking, predominates . . . It is essentially the realm to which the hackneyed phrase "wishful thinking" applies. If a person wants something to happen, but consciously says to himself "Don't be silly! It can't and won't happen", and dismisses the idea, the wish remains, but it is now in the unconscious, rather than the conscious field and has the freedom which results from being dismissed from the orderly class-room of deliberate thought . . . The medium may suddenly produce personal material relating to the sitter, tapping his unconscious mind and bringing to light hopes and desires of which perhaps he himself may be quite unaware.'

This does not mean that Miss Payne dismisses the possibility that the medium is sometimes transmitting a message coming from a discarnate spirit. She describes a highly significant incident in a séance she attended. It was an occasion on which the medium working there tapped thoughts which were in Miss Payne's own mind and also thoughts which she appeared to be receiving at that moment from a discarnate communicator. Miss Payne writes: 'At one séance a striking fact was that as my mind associated a number of memories and feelings with the material presented, the medium invariably gave these back to me, about half a minute later. It was as though she were on my mental track, and, as I thought a thing, she seemed to respond to that thought, and then echo it, as though she had received it from "the other side". Later in that séance, I was distinctly aware of another factor being introduced, and to my own perception this was a genuine element of telepathy from the mind of a person out of the body. My own thoughts and feelings were no longer the dominant part of the work. The medium went on quite steadily and acted as a bridge over which travelled the mental messages, but she was obviously unaware of any difference between *my* mind and the mind of the *communicator*. It bore out entirely the theory that the mind of a living person and the mind of a dead person operates in the same way. I summed that particular séance up as a very good demonstration of telepathy both from *this* side of death and the *other*.'

The following two stories illustrate this idea that the mind of a dead person may manifest itself at a séance in the same way that the mind of a living person manifests itself. The first of them is taken from Dr. and Mrs. Bendit's book *This World and That*, and it is told in the matter of fact and casual way in which these two writers describe what to another person would be an astonishing incident. Dr. Bendit begins by telling us that an intelligent middle-aged man had come to him for psychological help. He had recently lost an exceptionally gifted daughter who, after a very long illness, had died at the age of nineteen. The bereaved father was disconsolate and he had visited one medium after another in the hope of being able to get in touch with his daughter 'on the other side', but so far he had had no success. Dr. Bendit continues the story in the first person: 'I began by suggesting that he was probably frustrating himself by *demanding* of life that things should be otherwise than they were. I said that I thought the best course would be to make an inner act of acceptance of the physical loss of his daughter, coupled with a realization that life had mysterious purposes of its own, far beyond human reason. Such an act of faith – provided it was real and felt from the heart – would be far more likely to lead him to an intuitive sense that the link with his daughter was unbroken, save at the physical level. Even though he might not receive verbal messages of unproven authenticity, he might derive a much greater sense of satisfaction than any outer manifestations would give.

'During this conversation, I heard my wife return from a shopping expedition. I wanted to introduce her to my visitor, for reasons quite different from the purpose of his visit. I went to find her and discovered her shelling peas in the kitchen. She said she would come as soon as she had finished an urgent telephone call, which she did a few minutes later. After introductions had been made, I said, "Mr. C. has called because he has lost his daughter and wants very much to get into touch with her."

' "Don't tell me any more," interrupted my wife. She turned to my visitor.

' "This may very well be pure nonsense, but I tell you it for what it is worth. Was her name Margery, and was she nineteen when she died, and had she been ill for a long time?" She then described Margery, her features, temperament and outstanding capacities. She went on to say that while she was shelling peas before being fetched, a young girl suddenly appeared psychically and said, "I am Margery. Please tell my Daddy that I am trying to do what he wants. But he will not find me through séances. I want to communicate directly with him. Tell him not to be so impatient, but to go on trying to find me, even though it takes some time. Give him my love and tell him not to *think* too much, but to try and *feel* me."

'The father exclaimed, "That is what I wanted more

than anything else. It has given me confidence to go on my own way and not to listen to what other people tell me." '

Dr. Bendit makes the following comment on this story: 'This incident as between a father, his dead daughter, and a third person unknown to either, can, of course, be interpreted by the sceptic as an elaborate telepathic hallucination. In that case it would scarcely have conveyed to the outside person the sense of vivid and vital personality which the apparition gave, and seems much more likely to have been a real visit from a dead person who had been trying to find the right channel through which to put a message – like a person trying to find the right telephone number, but finding it difficult to get through because of confusion in the exchange; the exchange being, previously to this, a mixture of her father's and the medium's minds on which, so far, Margery had been able to make no impression.

'The interpretation of this particular episode seems to lean rather in the direction of its being what it purported to be, that is, a veridical touch from a dead person, alive and rational though out of the body, who found an adequate channel – through a trained psychic working in full consciousness, and not through a medium in a trance – to send a message to her father. Other explanations there may be and these should be borne in mind.'

The second story coming from an entirely different source illustrates the difficulty of deciding whether a message delivered by a medium can be explained telepathetically or whether it actually is what the

medium declares it to be, a message from the dead. It
is a story of some importance, for it is vouched for by
Dr. S. G. Soal, who has carried out such valuable work
on telepathy and precognition. Dr. Soal states that in
the year 1922 he had a sitting with a medium, a certain
Mrs. Blanche Cooper, and that during the course of
this she gave him the name of a boy whom he had
known, many years previously, at his old school. The
name of the boy was Gordon Davis. This boy had been
in the same class as Dr. Soal and he had brought to
the school and had displayed to Dr. Soal certain native
spears and arrows belonging to him. Afterwards Dr.
Soal had lost all touch with him, having met him only
once, namely in 1916 during the First World War. He
and Davis had then met accidentally at Shenfield
railway station, as military cadets, and had travelled
up to Liverpool Street together. Shortly afterwards the
two of them were drafted to the French Front and in
1920 Soal had heard that his old school friend had been
killed.

At a second session with the same medium in 1922,
Mrs. Cooper's control talked of Gordon Davis again
and gave a detailed description of what was said to be
Davis's home at that time. Then, three years later
(in 1925) Dr. Soal discovered that Davis had not been
killed but that he was still alive and was earning his
living as an estate agent in Southend. He also found
out that the description which Mrs. Cooper had given
of Davis's home did not tally with the house in which
he was living at the time of the séance but that it was
an entirely correct and detailed description of the
house into which he *subsequently* moved and in which

Dr. Soal later visited him. Fortunately Dr. Soal had kept the notes he had made at his sitting with Mrs. Cooper. They gave the following details of Mr. Davis's home:

1. A dark tunnel ran through the house. (The tunnel led into the garden.)
2. There was a veranda opposite it. (Actually it was a seaside shelter.)
3. It was in a street whose name began with two E's. (Mr. Davis's address was Eastern Esplanade.)
4. The pictures on the walls are of mountains and seas and one of them shows a road running between hills. (Correct.)
5. There is a black bird on the piano. (Actually a china ornament.)
6. There are two funny saucers on the walls and some curious vases. (Correct.)
7. There are two brass candlesticks, downstairs in the basement. (Correct.)
8. There is a woman and a child in the house. (Actually Dr. Soal had been unaware of the fact that Davis was married and had a child.)

It is noteworthy that Dr. Soal had always been particularly interested in the phenomenon of precognition and that precognition was playing an important role in this case also. Although at the time of the sittings with Mrs. Cooper, Davis possessed most of the articles described by her, he could not then have known that, at a later date, namely in January 1922, they would be so arranged that the ornamental bird was standing on the piano and the candlesticks relegated to the basement. It is fantastic that so much detailed information could have been precognized by Mrs. Cooper but less fantastic than the original idea that the communication had come from a discarnate spirit, the spirit of the still living Gordon Davis.

Dr. Osty's view on Mediumship

Dr. Eugène Osty was formerly in charge of the Institut Metaphysique International in Paris and his views about the way in which mediums work are of great importance. He prefers to use the term 'sensitive', for the word 'medium' is a limiting one and he believes that the 'sensitive' does much more than act as a communication channel for discarnate spirits. Dr. Osty reports that his own 'sensitives' worked in many different ways; some entered into different degrees of a trance state, whilst others gave their information in what appeared to be an ordinary state. All of them had this feature in common, that they never gave information about abstract or national events but always about small private events in the lives of the people with whom the 'sensitives' were in contact. Sometimes these private happenings were connected with greater historical events, such as wars, but only in so far as these historical events affected the individuals in question. For example, one of his 'sensitives' told her client prior to the outbreak of war that she saw him 'digging long galleries and giving orders to soldiers'.

Dr. Osty states that usually contact was established between the 'sensitive' and his client either by the latter's actual presence at the séance or else by means of some object belonging to him. When referring to the work of one of his best 'sensitives', a Mme Morel, Osty writes that 'the object placed in her hands availed to set her faculty in action, not by the fact of having belonged to such and such a person, but through having been *touched* by that person'. Dr. Osty arrived at this conclusion because if an object belonging to A were brought by B and were then given to C for transmission to Mme Morel, she invariably began by describing C, the last person to touch it. Then if she were asked to go back in time, Mme Morel would describe B and finally get back to A. This at first suggested that the touch of these people impressed something on to the material, but Osty is against this idea, and for the following reasons: (1) after the 'sensitive' had established connexion or *rapport* with the owner of the object by handling it, the object could be destroyed without interfering with the later stages of the experiment; (2) the material out of which the object was made was a matter of no importance; (3) the length of time it had been in A's possession made no difference; (4) the length of time that had elapsed since A had last touched it was equally unimportant. It would seem therefore that no knowledge is locked up within the object itself, but that its sole function is to direct the 'sensitive's' precognitive faculty in the right direction. It is difficult to state precisely how it does this but clairvoyant faculties are very precariously balanced and it sometimes happens that the destruction of the link between the medium and the individual with whom he or she was hoping to establish contact prevented these faculties from functioning. Dr. Osty sums up his own views on this subject as follows: 'When they work on an individual, distant in space or time, most percipients require an object coming from the individual to be cognized; with some few it is enough that the experimenter should be *thinking* of the person . . . Among percipients working in what seems a waking state, some only need their own mental impulse. Others excite the faculty by endless devices . . . Some look at the hands, some the writing, others use playing cards, a crystal ball, a glass of water, a candle, coffee grounds spilt on a plate, a heap of pins thrown on the carpet, etc. etc.'

After twelve years of experimenting with a number of different 'sensitives', Osty is fully convinced that there are people capable of foretelling the future of other people. He writes: 'I say the *future of other persons*, I do not say the future in general, which I have not verified personally. I am certain of this just as I am certain of what we call the earth, the sun, the stars, minerals, vegetables and animals. It is a fact verifiable by experiment against which our prejudgements will not avail, now that men of science have the courage to investigate the facts.'[1] No one could speak with greater assurance than this.

The Mediumship of Mrs. Piper

No medium has been more carefully studied than the famous American medium, Mrs. Piper, who remained under expert observation from 1886 until 1911. She emerged from all this testing with flying colours. As a young woman she had been quite unaware

[1] W. Osty, *Supernormal Faculties in Man*, 1923.

of the fact that she was a 'sensitive' and she only realized it after having had an accident from which she was taking a long time to recover. Because she was responding so slowly to her medical treatment she decided to seek help from a healer. During her second visit to him, she went into a state of semi-trance and later, having learnt how this could be done, she went into a semi-trance whenever she felt so inclined. On reaching this state her ordinary personality would disappear and she would begin to write and to speak of things of which she had previously had no knowledge. During her long subsequent career as a professional medium she claimed to have been controlled by a great many different spiritual guides. The first to act in this capacity was an Indian girl with the strange name of Chlorine and the second guide to appear was Dr. Phenuit, a French doctor. But Dr. Phenuit seems to have known very little about medicine and he had also forgotten how to speak and to write with ease in his native tongue. Like many other mediums, Mrs. Piper was extremely catholic in her choice of spiritual controls and during her long and distinguished professional career many famous people appear to have acted as her guides. The list included Bach, Longfellow and Mrs. Siddons. Amongst those who attended her séances and who were impressed by what they heard there were two female relatives of that great American psychologist, William James. They spoke to him afterwards of what they had seen and heard and although he laughed at what they reported about these spiritualistic performances, he consented to attend a séance himself. He kept his promise, and he also was struck by what happened at it. At a later date, he attended another session and was accompanied by Richard Hodgson, who at that time was acting as secretary to the newly formed American S.P.R. Both of these men possessed highly critical minds and Hodgson had previously displayed a special talent for unmasking trickery. The measures which he now adopted for detecting fraud in Mrs. Piper were remarkably thorough. A number of detectives were engaged to watch her house, her family and Mrs. Piper herself, in order to make quite sure that no inquiries were being made by agents acting on her behalf, and investigating the circumstances and the private lives of the many people who now attended her séances. Nothing of this kind could be discovered, nor was it ever discovered during the many years that Mrs. Piper was kept under close scrutiny. Having satisfied themselves of her honesty, William James and Richard Hodgson decided that Mrs. Piper should pay a visit to the British S.P.R. This visit to England was actually made in 1889 and after staying for the first few weeks of her visit with the psychologist, Dr. F. W. Myers, Mrs. Piper became the guest of the well-known scientist, Sir Oliver Lodge. He adopted the following special measures in order to prevent her from acquiring any knowledge of himself, of his family and of his friends. A completely new set of domestic servants was specially engaged and all the family albums, bibles, photos and other sources of information were locked up in a cupboard. A search of Mrs. Piper's luggage was made whilst she was out, and everybody introduced to her was introduced under a pseudonym. Having discovered nothing suspicious,

Sir Oliver Lodge decided to write a letter to an uncle of his asking him to send something which had previously belonged to this uncle's twin brother who had been dead for twenty years. A gold watch was chosen and sent, and when it was handed, without comment, to Mrs. Piper in her semi-trance state, she replied almost immediately that the watch had previously belonged to an uncle of Sir Oliver Lodge's and that he had a name like 'Jerry'. On being encouraged to say more about this said uncle, Mrs. Piper narrated several incidents of his boyhood, the correctness of which was afterwards confirmed by his twin brother still alive. She gave a description of Jerry's swimming in a creek, of his being nearly drowned, of his slaughtering a cat in a meadow known by the name of 'Smith's Field' and of his having possessed a skin which 'looked like the dried skin of a snake'. Lodge himself was entirely ignorant of all these incidents in the life of his dead uncle, so that if Mrs. Piper had managed to obtain information about them telepathically from the mind of some living person, it must have been from the mind of Sir Oliver Lodge's surviving uncle.

After further investigation of Mrs. Piper and of her mediumistic methods, the British S.P.R. came to the same conclusions as those which had been reached previously in America, namely, that she was honest and that her mediumship was of a very high order. The Society was less favourably impressed by Mrs. Piper's control, Dr. Phenuit, and doubtless they were relieved when the French doctor, who knew so little French and even less medicine, was replaced by another spirit control, a Mr. Pelham, who when alive had been a friend of the American investigator Richard Hodgson. This new spirit guide did not entirely eliminate Dr. Phenuit from the spiritual field but when the latter appeared he and his supplanter, Richard Hodgson, seem to have worked together amicably, Dr. Phenuit talking briskly on one subject, whilst Mr. Pelham continued writing busily on an entirely different subject.

A long and careful report on Mrs. Piper was eventually drawn up and edited by Mrs. Sedgwick. In it she expressed the opinion that although Mrs. Piper's controls were clearly dramatic constructions of her own mind, there were good reasons for believing that a 'genuine communicator' existed somewhere in the background. Mrs. Sedgwick's actual words on this subject are as follows: 'Of course, communication with the dead, when it occurs, must imply a real communicator in the background, but the point is that this does not necessitate either the dramatic communicator or the control being other than phases or elements of Mrs. Piper. Nor does it exclude the possibility that the dramatic communicator is a fiction or a dream or a hallucination of the control, each of which things it sometimes appears to be. That it is with phases or elements – centres of consciousness – of Mrs. Piper, and not with entities independent of her, that the sitter is in direct communication seems to me, for the reasons given, to be the hypothesis which best fits the facts, so far as we know them . . . And it is also a hypothesis against which no valid arguments have, so far as I have seen, been adduced.'[1]

[1] Quoted by F. W. H. Myers in *Human Personality*.

Of Mrs. Piper's complete honesty there can be no doubt. Never has a medium been more carefully watched and followed than she was watched and followed, and seldom have so many men and women of good repute testified to the reliability of anyone as those who testified to the good faith of Mrs. Piper. William James wrote the following of her: 'During the years 1892–6 inclusive, I exercised a yet closer supervision of Mrs. Piper's trances than I had done in previous years, continuing to take all the precautions that I could, as regards the introduction of persons as strangers. This period was marked by a notable evolution of the quality of the trance results, beginning early in 1892. The character of the manifestation changed with the development of automatic writing in the trance, and with what was alleged to be the continual rendering of active assistance by the communicator I have called G.P. (George Pelham). As a result of this it appears that communicators were able to express their thoughts directly through writing by Mrs. Piper's hand, instead of conveying them more dimly and partially through Phenuit as intermediary.' Two years later William James added to this testimonial to Mrs. Piper the following words: 'Dr. Hodgson considers that the hypothesis of fraud cannot be seriously maintained. I agree with him absolutely.'[1]

Mrs. Piper's Failure

Mrs. Piper must be accounted an extremely reliable and successful medium but in spite of this she had her failures. The most outstanding of these was her inability

[1] Quoted by F. W. H. Myers in *Human Personality*.

to communicate the contents of a sealed letter left by Dr. Hodgson. Little is known about the private life of Dr. Hodgson beyond the fact that he had promised to do his best to communicate the contents of a sealed letter to his friends after his death. He died a few years later and Mrs. Piper claimed to have got in touch with him, but her efforts to communicate what lay within the sealed envelope were a complete failure. This is a test to which several good mediums have been subjected and, so far as I know, none of them have yet passed it. The prize for passing it – there is said to be a prize – has never been won.

Telepathy and Communication from the Dead

To what extent can telepathic communication with *living* minds account for the intimate knowledge of past, and apparently forgotten, events revealed by such a medium as Mrs. Piper? This is a question which in these circumstances always obtrudes itself and sternly demands of us some answer. It must be remembered that telepathy and clairvoyance are now much more widely accepted than they were in the days when Mrs. Sedgwick and William James were testifying to the honesty of Mrs. Piper, and it is, of course, possible that telepathy may have accounted for some of Mrs. Piper's knowledge of past and seemingly forgotten events. But it is unlikely that it provides a satisfactory explanation for everything happening at her séances. Professor Broad has discussed this subject in an article published in the Proceedings of the S.P.R. and he sums up his views on it as follows: 'There are also cases in which it is alleged that a medium produces automatic script purporting to be written under the control of the spirit of a certain deceased human being, and undoubtedly in his highly characteristic handwriting, although she has never seen, either in original or in reproduction, any specimen of his manuscript. I do not know whether any such cases are well attested, but if they be, they fall under the same category as the dead voice cases, some of which certainly appear to be so. Now it seems to me that any attempt to explain these phenomena by reference to telepathy amongst the living, stretches the word telepathy until it becomes meaningless . . . *Prima facie* such phenomena are strong evidence for the persistence, after a man's death, of something which carries traces of his experience, habits and skills.'

The Significance of the Whole

The time has come for summarizing the conclusions reached in the foregoing chapters and for relating, so far as we are able to do this, the phenomena we have been studying to our conception of the human mind. But there is a preliminary question which must first be faced, a question which G. N. M. Tyrell asks in the final chapter of his book, *The Human Personality*. If telepathy, precognition and clairvoyance are genuine phenomena why is there so much doubt about them, and why do so many people still regard them as being only the production of the imagination? It is not as though man had suddenly become aware of such phenomena as telepathy and prophetic dreams, for he has been studying them and marvelling at them for over six thousand years. Why is there still so much scepticism concerning their genuine character?

One of the explanations of this is that we live in a scientific age in which nothing is accepted that has not received the ratification of the scientists. Now the paranormal phenomena of the human mind we have been studying cannot be investigated in the same way that physical phenomena are investigated for they belong to a different order. In the physical sciences we are dealing with events which can be carefully observed and which can often be measured. This means that they can be verified by means of controlled experiments capable of being repeated by other experimenters under more or less similar conditions. But when we are investigating events taking place neither in the physical world outside ourselves nor in the more conscious regions of our minds, these methods of verification cannot be used. We are dealing here with phenomena over which we have little or no control and which are not open to direct observation. We cannot see the workings of the unconscious mind; we only see the results of these workings when they are manifesting themselves on the more conscious levels of the mind. All that we are able to do in the way of exercising control over these elusive phenomena is to encourage the human subject we are investigating to get himself into the psychological state in which the phenomena are more likely to occur. And, as we have seen in the preceding chapters, if we make too many demands on our subject or expect him to repeat the experiments so often that he becomes bored with them, the elusive phenomena we are studying fail to manifest themselves. In short the human mind cannot be examined in precisely the same way as we examine a physical object.

The next question to be answered is whether the evidence in favour of the existence of extra-sensory perception is of such an overwhelmingly satisfactory nature that we are now compelled to accept it. The question has been put in this way because our minds are seldom, if ever, neutral on the subject of extra-sensory perception but display an obvious bias, either for or against it. Yet when we come to examine this question, in as detached a manner as possible, there is nothing at all absurd in the *a priori* idea that Nature does not come to an end at that point at which our senses cease to register anything happening, even when our senses have been rendered more sensitive by the addition of scientific instruments. As Tyrell has put it: 'The order of existence with which our senses make us familiar is not the *whole*. There is an *elsewhere* in which the order is different. We do not come across this *elsewhere* by exploring the external world . . . It is only by looking into the personality of man that we discover the existence of it.'

Because of this inherent bias against the acceptance of extra-sensory perception many people demand overwhelming evidence before they will even consider its existence. Their bias is so strong that they are not even willing to look at the immense amount of painstaking work which has been done on this subject during the last twenty years. Now, they are quite justified in demanding severe tests for phenomena which seem to conflict with the findings of science, but their demands are often so excessive as to be ridiculous. In 1952, Dr. Lucien Warner, an American biologist, quoted the opinions of a number of different American psychologists on the subject of Psychical Research and the following are two samples of them.

'What are the quirks of personality that lead an otherwise scientific psychologist to continue to waste his time on so unrewarding a field of inquiry?'

'One is forced to the conclusion that there is something about this problem that leads the people who are attracted to it to come to false positive conclusions.'[1]

---

[1] Quoted by Rosalind Heywood in *The Sixth Sense*.

It is necessary to examine the evidence for and against the existence of extra-sensory perception very carefully, not because it is ridiculous to imagine the existence of an *elsewhere* beyond the reach of our senses but because many supposed cases of telepathy are capable of being explained in other ways. They may either be explained by pure accident or else they may be the result only of careful observation and intuitive guessing. It is astonishing what two clever performers, such as the Piddington couple, managed to do by these means and it is equally surprising what the television star Chan Canasta is contriving to do by special methods at the present time. Practically all public demonstrations of telepathy are carried out with the help of pre-arranged codes and of clever intuitive guesses and it is very easy to be deceived into accepting these demonstrations as genuine examples of telepathy and clairvoyance.

When all cases of a doubtful nature have been eliminated there still remains, in the opinion of the author, a residue which cannot be explained otherwise than in terms of extra-sensory perception. The statistical evidence obtained in favour of this appears to me to be overwhelming. It is true that Mr. Spenser Brown has published a book entitled *Probability and Scientific Inference* in which he casts doubt on the reliability of this statistical evidence, but having received Dr. Soal's personal assurance on the subject I still retain my faith in the statistical support we now have for clairvoyance, telepathy and precognition.

The second problem with which we are faced is that of finding a place for extra-sensory perception in our general scheme of thought. In this age of science we all think very much as the scientists do. This being so, we soon realize the stern fact that telepathy and precognition are running counter to what Professor Broad has called 'the basic limiting principles of ordinary thought', which is only another way of saying that they are running counter to the basic limiting principles of *scientific* thought. In order therefore to find a place in our thinking for extra-sensory perception a certain amount of reconstruction of thought becomes necessary. Amongst the changes which will have to be made in it is the abandonment of the basic scientific principle that a cause must always precede in time its effect, for in precognition the effect is in advance of its cause. Dare we take such liberties as this with the scientific methods? In the opinion of the author, we dare. The scientists are quite justified in placing the emphasis they do on mechanism, but all causations are not necessarily mechanistic in character. Aristotle, who may be looked upon as being the grandfather of Western science, clearly recognized this fact and he taught that a cause may lie out there in the future in the form of a *goal* or a *purpose*. It is true that *teleology* or purposive action has been highly unpopular in the Western sciences and even in those departments of science in which the idea of purpose is particularly needed, the sciences of life, for in the opinion of the author 'life' is inherently goal-seeking and purposeful. Every living thing is an organized system which is developing in an orderly fashion towards a definite goal. The goal towards which it strives is that of becoming a mature individual and of surviving for as long as possible. It is not only legitimate, but it is also necessary, for the biologist to include such concepts as memory, drives and purposive actions in his explanation of living processes, for these processes cannot be explained in terms of antecedent causes and of machinery alone. Goal-seeking and directiveness should be regarded as being two of the distinctive characteristics of the process we call life.

These two ways of looking at causes, the *mechanistic* and the *purposive* or teleological should be available to us and it is entirely natural that the scientist should have favoured, and should continue to favour the former method of explaining things. The physicist is in the vanguard of scientific progress and the physicist is a mechanist who takes it for granted that all physical phenomena have been brought about by causes which precede effects. If he did not assume this he would be unable to predict things and prediction is an all-important item in the scientist's work. At present he is quite unable to abandon the basic idea which has brought him so much profit, his mechanistic model of the Universe, even when he has to deal with living things. Nevertheless, there is a growing tendency amongst biologists to express heterodox views and to recognize the obvious fact that purposefulness is a characteristic of all living things.

Let us accept, for the time being, the genuine nature of the phenomena we have been studying and let us examine certain aspects of them. A question presents itself when we consider in greater detail the phenomenon of precognition. Let us suppose that a person 'precognizes' a disaster looming in his future, a disaster

which is of so serious a nature that it will destroy him.
The question arises whether or not, having been thus
forewarned, he will be able to adopt measures to avoid
it. We shall not embark on a preliminary discussion
on the subject of determinism versus indeterminism in
the field of human action, for that would be of no
profit to us. We shall assume what everybody does
assume in everyday life, that we all possess a *modicum*
of what is known as 'free will'. Having taken this for
granted we can return to the question whether or not
a forewarned person, by taking adequate measures,
could avoid the fate which he has 'precognized'. Let
us take as an example, Abraham Lincoln's dream that
he, the President of the United States, was soon to be
assassinated. Might it not have been possible for him
to have avoided his fate by shunning all public
ceremonies and by doubling the security precautions
in force for safeguarding the life of an American
President? The answer is 'no', for there lurks a fallacy
in the question itself. If Abraham Lincoln had taken
the necessary precautions, and if they had proved
successful, then assassination would not have been an
event in his life, and this being so he could not have
precognized it. All that could have been precognized
by him, had he adopted successful methods for his own
protection, would have been that he was about to be
subjected to annoying inconveniences for a period of
time and that in the end the precautions he had taken
would turn out to have been quite unnecessary. In
other words, a person can only precognize future
events in his own life if these events are of such a nature
that it is quite unnecessary for him to take steps to

prevent them. There is no reason, of course, why a person should not precognize important and dangerous events in *another* person's life, provided that neither he nor the person in question interferes with what is expected to happen later.

Another obstacle to the acceptance of precognition is that it seems to entail an acceptance of the idea that the future already exists. For if the future did not already exist, then how could it have been apprehended? In an article dealing with the logical and scientific implications of precognition, Mr. L. C. Robinson has tackled this problem, and he points out 'that what are immediately prehended are not the future events themselves . . . In precognition the present perception or awareness is merely of contemporary images referable in thought to the future.'[1] An acceptance of precognition undoubtedly requires of us that we should revise our views, not only of our perception of time but of time itself. That this is necessary has been recognized by many writers on this subject, notably by Professors Broad and Price, and by Dunne, the author of *An Experiment with Time*. The revision which has usually been suggested is that we should postulate not one but several dimensions of time and should abandon our customary lineal conception of it. L. C. Robinson seems to agree with this for he writes: 'The central difficulty in any study of the nature of precognition is in regard to the status of the future. Considerations compel us logically to the view that what appears to be future is not really future in the sense of being non-existent, and we cannot but hold that there is some-

[1] *Journal for Psychical Research*, vol. 39, no. 693.

thing delusive in ordinary perception with its successive phases of past, present and future . . . Whatever its uses may be as a mathematical conception, time is not in reality a unilinear irreversible series of events flowing in one direction only, from the past to the future, but must be regarded as being rather a *totum simul* in which past, present and future co-exist, though they appear, to normal consciousness, to be successive phases in a temporal flow.'

Personal experience shows us that past, present and future may co-exist for us at the same moment of time. 'In the specious present or the time-span of ordinary consciousness we have, as it were, a *duration-block* in which successive events with distinctions of before-and-after are also manifestly contemporary in time. Its reality cannot be questioned as it is not a matter of inference but of direct experience. Its temporal extensity is estimated to range from about half a second to as much as four seconds . . . This variability of the time-span of consciousness, together with its unique feature of being an enduring present in which past, present and future co-exist, albeit only momentarily, carries with it an implication of profound significance to the whole question of precognition.'

Robinson suggests that if we could extend this duration-block a little, we might be able to prehend an event farther ahead of us than we usually prehend. He points out that this is very far from being a novel idea for in discussing the limitations of human knowledge, Bertrand Russell often speaks of 'a complex of compresence'. He means by that phrase a moment of experience in which past, present and future are all 'compresent' or apprehended altogether. So also did F. W. H. Myers write, many years ago, that it might be possible to extend artificially this period of compresent past, present and future.

Precognition and the Field Theory

Dr. Gardner Murphy has sought to overcome the difficulty occasioned by precognition in an entirely different manner. He believes that all that is required of us in order to explain the phenomena of telepathy and precognition is that we should extend the use of the 'field-theory' into the realms of psychology and parapsychology. The field-theory to which he is referring began to take shape towards the end of the last century when that very great physicist, Clerk Maxwell, put forward what was then a novelty, the idea of an electro-magnetic field. Up till that time physicists had been in the habit of describing everything in terms of the activities of localized atoms and they had never thought in broader terms of patterns of events and of the behaviour of wholes. But from Clerk Maxwell's time onward attention was transferred from small *local* units to much larger units in which energies or particles could be looked upon as being organized into 'patterns of events'. It has also been recognized that structural wholes of this kind may well be more than the sums of their parts.

The idea of fields or patterns of events has now spread into other departments of science. For example, the biologist, Paul Weiss, has taken cells from one part of a developing embryo and has grafted them on to some other part of it and he has thereby shown that

grafted cells can change their nature in response to
the requirements of the whole. For example, skin cells
may develop into muscle cells and muscle cells into
nerve cells, showing that the field, or structural whole,
exercises control over what is happening within
different areas of it. The same idea has been applied to
sociology and there are those who believe that human
beings can be organized into highly complex units
which may be greater than the sum of the individuals
constituting them. By extending this field-theory into
parapsychology, Gardner Murphy believes that we
can explain much that is obscure in the working of the
Psi factor in man. He suggests that we are responding
automatically to environmental stimuli for 99.9 per cent
of our time but that occasionally a leak of time-space-
energy occurs in this closed system so that we suddenly
become aware of something outside the field of our
environment. In Gardner Murphy's opinion these
revealing flashes (many of them occur amongst subjects
engaged in the card-guessing experiments) are an
indication that man possesses, at a deeper level, the
capacity to establish contact with all space and with
all time. He is of the opinion that had we not become
psychologically estranged and insulated from one
another in the West, so that we are no longer open to
one another, these flashes of extra-sensory perception
would have been much commoner events.

The Field-Theory and the Level of Consciousness

It is possible to extend the idea of 'fields' into the
realm of consciousness and to talk about different fields
or areas of consciousness, for the area of awareness, as

well as its intensity, differs on different levels. In the ordinary waking state we have our own restricted personal field of consciousness, but in contemplation the 'ego' of everyday life may be transcended, so that the field of consciousness widens, and we are no longer isolated individuals but parts of a great Whole. It is this Unity of Consciousness which the mystic finds it so difficult to explain to others who have not experienced it, and it is this which the Upanishad is attempting to put into words when it exclaims: 'Indivisible but as if divided in being'. All Consciousness is One but in our ordinary waking state it seems to be divided into innumerable parts, each person possessing a separate consciousness of his own.

Before leaving this important subject of higher levels of consciousness it is necessary to make sure that no confusion has been occasioned by discussing the factor of consciousness in a chapter concerned with extra-sensory perception. It must be kept clearly in mind that the phenomena of telepathy, clairvoyance and precognition are activities of the Unconscious and not of the Superconscious mind, for in higher states of consciousness the concept of 'before' and 'after' entirely disappear. This being so, precognition is more likely to occur in states of *diminished* awareness. We have to accept the fact that many errors are made in the West about the all-important phenomenon of consciousness. For example, there is a common misconception that mystics are people who sit about in a semi-conscious state conjuring up dreams and oblivious of all else. But the truth is the very reverse of this. The mystic is a man who has subjected his mind to very severe disciplining and he is not only aware of himself and of his surroundings but he is much more fully aware of these things than are other people. This means that the contemplative is very far from being an idle dreamer. He is a man who, by years of practice, has trained his attention and disciplined his thinking. As a result of this he has made himself capable of reaching a higher level of consciousness and of receiving, in this state, direct knowledge. And, so far as I know, the psychological state of the contemplative is not one which is likely to be conducive to extra-sensory activities in his Unconscious Mind.

Contact between the Unconscious Regions of Different Minds

The idea that Consciousness is One does not alter the fact that our minds are multiple and that each of us possesses a separate mind of his own. Nevertheless, there is a growing feeling amongst parapsychologists that on their lower and *Unconscious* levels individual minds come into more intimate contact with one another than we formerly believed them to do. This permits of different minds communicating with one another by means of telepathy. Sometimes we have a feeling that we have established a very close relationship with another mind. In moments of deep relaxation and of freedom from the compulsions of the 'ego' we feel and understand one another in a way in which we did not feel and understand one another before. It is as though we had established a direct *rapport* with one another in the depths of our being, so that there is no longer any need for an interchange of words.

The Final Question

The last question which needs answering is whether a recognition of the genuineness of the psychic phenomena discussed in this book is likely to lead to confusion in other spheres of thought and particularly in our views of the universe in which we live. At first sight an acceptance of the phenomena of telepathy, clairvoyance and precognition would seem to entail a contradiction of the established laws of science but only because we have made the unwarrantable assumption that everything which happens in our experience must of necessity happen in that particular world order with which we are most familiar, the world order of time and space. As Tyrell has put it: 'If we admit a region *outside* the familiar world order for paranormal events to happen in, there is no longer any reason to suppose that they contradict or interfere with the laws of nature.' By the word 'outside', Tyrell means some *locus* for events which lies beyond our customary world of time and space and, as we have already seen, telepathy – if it exists – has no regard for space. So also has precognition equally little regard for time and this being so, these phenomena must belong to an order of existence 'outside' of the world of space and time.

This does not mean that the world in which these psychic phenomena are occurring is a world of a *supernatural* character. On the contrary, the phenomena in question are entirely natural phenomena in the sense that they belong to an *ordered whole* but a whole which is likely to be dominated by laws which differ from those controlling the more familiar space-time world. We have given to the word 'Nature' far too restricted a meaning, applying it only to those aspects of Nature which our special senses are capable of revealing to us. But it would be ridiculous for us to imagine that there exists nothing beyond the reach of these very limited sense organs of ours and that the model of the world which we have constructed on the basis of the sense-data received from it is in any way a complete model of it. There is a great deal in Nature which is not represented in this model because it lies in the area of the extra-sensory. So also shall we have to restore to Nature many of those attributes of which we have been dispoiling her from the days of Locke and Newton onwards. As Whitehead has pointed out, Newton's methodology for physics proved an overwhelming success, but the forces which he introduced left Nature still without any meaning or value. And science has not only deprived Nature of meaning and value, but it has also stripped her of all life and mind. These will have to be returned to her sooner or later, for 'a dead and mindless Nature aims at nothing' and can have no meaning. The scientists conduct a piecemeal examination of Nature, abstracting from her those qualities which they are able to scrutinize and measure and neglecting all the rest. But Nature is a Unity and this method of abstracting certain items from that Unity and of considering them in a state of isolation is highly misleading.

One of the most disastrous of the many abstractions made by the scientists is that for which Descartes was mainly responsible, the abstraction which has led to a complete separation between life, mind and matter. Life, mind and matter are not three separate things which have somehow or other managed to come together. They are closely linked entities in that great patterned process which we call Nature. This means also that the whole Cosmos is alive. There will be no difficulty in reconciling the conclusion which has been reached that telepathy, clairvoyance and precognition are genuine phenomena with the established laws of science, provided that we recognize the nature of these scientific laws. The scientist starts his investigations by making certain abstractions from the whole and, as Whitehead is continually reminding us – an abstraction entails an omission of part of the truth. This means that the established laws of science are laws of a strictly limited nature.

The philosopher who has been quoted most frequently in this book is A. N. Whitehead and I frankly admit that he has had a stronger influence over my thinking than has any other Western writer. Whitehead's conception of the universe resembles in many respects Hegel's conception of it. He sees it as a complete and indivisible whole, but there is a difference between his and Hegel's way of looking at it. Whereas Hegel's universe is static and complete, Whitehead's universe is a living and an 'evolving universe, ever plunging into the creative advance'. It is living, not so much in the sense of being a single living organism, 'but living in the sense in which the process of the harmonious development of mutually *prehending* organisms may be said to be alive'.[1]

The word *prehending* used by Whitehead is of special

---

[1] A. N. Whitehead, *Nature and Life.*

interest to us, for, as we shall see later, it embodies an idea which is very similar, if not identical, with the idea of 'extra-sensory perception'. According to Whitehead, it is essential that the many members of the society of evolving organisms which constitute the universe should maintain a very close relationship with one another. Not only are they working in close collaboration with each other but they are affecting each other's nature all the time, and Whitehead has coined this word 'prehension' to denote the close inter-action and inter-relationship which exists between the various members of the society of evolving organisms. This term has been obtained from the two words 'apprehension' and 'comprehension' and it retains much of the meaning of these two parent words. Miss Emmet, an authority on Whitehead's philosophy, defines *prehension* as 'the grasping by one actual entity of some aspect or part of other actual entities and appropriating them in the formation of its own nature'. Whitehead tells us that *prehension* is more allied to feeling than to thought and he likens it to that strange faculty by means of which we sometimes sense the presence of another sentient being, without our special sense-organs having played any part in the recognition. According to Whitehead, every entity is 'related to' and 'prehends' everything else in the universe, however remote the relationship between them may be. He also makes use of the term *negative prehension*. In view of the fact that each entity in the universe is that particular entity and not something else, a previous process of selection of characteristics must have taken place. In other words, the entity in question must have previously accepted and developed certain qualities (positive prehension) and have rejected other qualities (negative prehension). As a result of 'prehension', a faculty closely allied, if not identical with direct extra-sensory perception, a choice has been made and choice indicates the existence of some degree of intelligence in the entity. But this idea that all things possess their intelligence, should occasion no difficulty for what, after all, is intelligence but the capacity of an entity to make meaningful adjustments to its environment. This is no new idea and Whitehead quotes a passage from Sir Francis Bacon's *Natural History*, which strongly suggests that Bacon not only attributed mind and intelligence to Nature but that he shared Whitehead's view that everything *prehends*, and takes stock of everything else in Nature:

'It is certain that all bodies whatsoever, though they have no sense, yet they have perception; for when one body is applied to another, there is a kind of election to embrace that which is agreeable, and to exclude or expel that which is ingrate; and whether the body be alterant or altered, evermore a perception precedeth operation; for else all bodies would be like one to another. And sometimes this perception in some kind of bodies is far more subtile than sense; so that sense is but a dull thing in comparison of it; we see a weather glass will find the least difference of the weather in heat or cold, when we find it not. And this perception is sometimes at a distance, as well as upon the touch; as when the loadstone draweth iron; or flame naphtha of Babylon, a great distance off. It is therefore a subject of a very noble inquiry, to inquire of the more subtile perceptions; for it is another key to open nature, as well as the sense; and sometimes better.'

After quoting these lines, Whitehead expresses the opinion that Bacon's attitude to Nature embodied more fundamental truths than did the materialistic and mechanistic descriptions of Nature which were becoming fashionable in the scientific literature of the Elizabethan Age. If we accept therefore Bacon's and Whitehead's view that Nature as a whole is intelligent, purposeful, alive and self-creative, then there is no longer need for us to do violence to our reason and to assert, as nineteenth-century scientists frequently asserted, that we human beings are the sole representatives of mind and intelligence in this vast universe. Nor will it any longer be necessary for us to find a solution to the problem of how, from a dead, mindless and mechanistic world, there emerged such an anomaly as a truth-seeking man. Long ago in ancient Greece, Zeno put this same question to his fellow philosophers and immediately returned an answer to it. He asked 'Why not admit that the world is a *living* and a *rational* being since it produces animate and rational entities?' Why not indeed? When we look up at the stars on a clear starlit night is it not a little bit arrogant on our part to assume, as we are inclined to do, that in all that immensity and grandeur we, the tiny inhabitants of this earth, are the sole representatives of consciousness, mind and intelligence?

Man's views about himself have been as subject to change as have his views about the universe and a rhythmic quality is noticeable in his thinking, so that he swings from one extreme to another extreme.

Nietzsche has drawn our attention to the changes in man's opinion of himself as revealed in the different periods of ancient Greek Culture. The official view of man was expressed by the majority of the philosophers living in the classical age of Greece and also in its art, its rituals and its religion. This official account of man represented him as endowed with a god-like reason which made him master, not only of external Nature but also of the irrational forces of passion which dwelt within him. Nietzsche called this the Appollonian attitude to man. But alongside this official view of man there existed another, less optimistic and less flattering view of him which Nietzsche calls the Dionysian attitude to man. According to this darker current of ideas, man was not standing god-like and impartial above the level of Nature, but he was himself, a product of Nature and consequently subject to the same compulsions and laws as those to which Nature herself was subject. It was true that man was endowed with reason but even at its best reason was a fallible instrument, helpful to man in finding his way about in the world around him but of little use to him when he sought to penetrate the dark mysteries which lay within himself. Of this inner and bewildering world some understanding might occasionally come to him from flashes of his intuition but he would never learn to know himself by the use of his intellect alone.

This second and Dionysian view was favoured by Aristotle but not by Plato and it is becoming popular again in the present time. Brilliant though the achievements of man's intellect have been, more and more people are beginning to realize that man is controlled by his feelings rather than by his reason. As Whitehead has put it, man is not primarily a rational being, but is a being who is 'subject to fits of rationality' and our study of man's Unconscious Mind has strengthened this Dionysian view of him. It has revealed to us a number of new and unsuspected forces operating in the darker regions of his mind, forces which, unbeknown to himself, exercise their influence on his thinking and his actions. This all goes to show that the factors involved in man's thinking and behaviour are far more numerous and more complicated than we formerly believed them to be.

INDEX

INDEX

71 72 73 74   12 11 10 9 8 7 6 5 4 3 2 1